C for FORTRAN Programmers

C for FORTRAN Programmers

T. D. Brown, Jr.

Silicon Press
25 Beverly Road
Summit, NJ 07901, USA

Silicon Press
25 Beverly Road
Summit, NJ 07901, USA

Printing 9 8 7 6 5 4 3 2 1   Year 94 93 92 91 90
First Edition

IBM is a registered trademark of IBM.
Turbo C is a registered trademark of Borland International, Inc.
MS is a trademark of the Microsoft Corporation.
UNIX is a registered trademark of AT&T.
VAX is a registered trademark of DEC.
Apple is a trademark of Apple Computers.

Library of Congress Cataloging-in-Publication Data

Brown, T. D.
  C for FORTRAN Programmers / T. D. Brown, Jr. -- 1st ed.
     p.   cm.
  Includes bibliographical references.
  Includes index.
  ISBN 0-929306-01-5
  1. C (Computer program language)   I. Title
  QA76.73.C15B774   1990   89-10810
005.13´3--dc20   CIP

BOOK EXAMPLES ON DISKETTE

For a diskette (in MS-DOS format) containing the source for the programs given in this book, send US $25.00 (includes shipping and handling) to

Silicon Press
25 Beverly Road
Summit, NJ 07901, USA

CONTENTS

PREFACE ix

CHAPTER 1   INTRODUCTION.. 1
                 1. GENERAL COMMENTS ABOUT C 1
                 2. A QUICK TOUR OF THE C LANGUAGE 2
                 3. FINAL COMMENTS 24
                 4. EXERCISES 25

CHAPTER 2   FORTRAN FACILITIES PRESENT IN C
                        & VICE VERSA.. 27
                 1. GENERAL COMMENTS ABOUT C 2 7
                 2. BASICS OF C 28
                 3. FUNDAMENTAL TYPES 32
                 4. DERIVED TYPES 35
                 5. OPERATORS & EXPRESSIONS 42
                 6. VARIABLE INITIALIZATION 55
                 7. STATEMENTS 56
                 8. FUNCTIONS 60
                 9. INPUT/OUTPUT 61
                 10. COMMONLY USED INPUT/OUTPUT FUNCTIONS 64
                 11. ERROR TRAPPING 65
                 12. PROGRAM TERMINATION 65
                 13. EXERCISES 66

CHAPTER 3   C FACILITIES NOT IN FORTRAN................................. 67
                 1. C PREPROCESSOR 67
                 2. TYPES 67
                 3. OPERATORS 78
                 4. STATEMENTS 79
                 5. FUNCTIONS 86
                 6. STORAGE CLASSES 86
                 7. SIGNAL HANDLING 88

8. EXERCISES 89

CHAPTER 4   **FUNCTIONS** 91
1. FUNCTION DEFINITIONS 91
2. FUNCTION PROTOTYPES (DECLARATIONS) 93
3. FUNCTION CALLS 94
4. ARGUMENT PASSING 95
5. FUNCTION RESULT & COMPLETION 97
6. RECURSION 97
7. STATIC VARIABLES 99
8. COMMUNICATION BETWEEN FUNCTIONS 100
9. FUNCTION NAMES AS ARGUMENTS 101
10. VARIABLE NUMBER OF ARGUMENTS 102
11. INDEPENDENT COMPILATION 103
12. INTERRUPT (SIGNAL) HANDLING 104
13. PROGRAM TERMINATION 106
14. ACCESSING OPERATING SYSTEM FACILITIES 106
15. CALLING ROUTINES WRITTEN IN OTHER LANG. 107
16. EXAMPLES 107
17. EXERCISES 111

CHAPTER 5   **POINTERS** 113
1. VOID POINTERS 113
2. ALLOCATING & DEALLOCATING STORAGE 114
3. POINTER ARITHMETIC 115
4. LISTS: AN EXAMPLE OF POINTER USE 115
5. POINTERS & ARRAYS 117
6. DYNAMIC ARRAYS 120
7. EXAMPLES 121
8. EXERCISES 131

CHAPTER 6   **C PREPROCESSOR** 133
1. MACRO DEFINITIONS 133
2. SETS: AN EXAMPLE OF PARAMETERIZED MACROS 140
3. FILE INCLUSION 142
4. CONDITIONAL COMPILATION 143
5. AVOIDING MULTIPLE FILE INCLUSIONS 145
6. EXERCISES 146

CHAPTER 7   **LARGE EXAMPLES** 147
1. TEMPERATURE DISTRIBUTION 147
2. THE BANK TELLER PROGRAM 150
3. THE TEXT FORMATTER 160

4. EXERCISES 167

CHAPTER 8 **FORTRAN FACILITIES NOT IN C**................................... 169

APPENDIX **C LIBRARY FUNCTIONS**.. 173
1. CHARACTER PROCESSING 174
2. MATH 175
3. NON-LOCAL JUMPS 178
4. SIGNAL HANDLING 178
5. VARIABLE ARGUMENTS 179
6. INPUT/OUTPUT 179
7. GENERAL UTILITY 192
8. STRING PROCESSING 195

BIBLIOGRAPHY 199

INDEX 201

PREFACE

This book is written especially for fluent FORTRAN programmers interested in learning C. It is not a beginning C book, for it assumes that the reader is familiar with basic programming concepts and wants to learn, not just the C syntax, but how to program well in C. The goal is not to teach the reader how to write FORTRAN programs in C but to teach C programming concepts. The book focuses on effective C programming using C programming paradigms.

FORTRAN has the honor of being the world's first high-level programming language. It was designed in the 1950s at IBM by a team led by John Backus. The original FORTRAN has been revised several times with each revision adding new concepts to the language. The FORTRAN discussed in this book is ANSI FORTRAN 77 which is a revised version of FORTRAN 66 (popularly known as FORTRAN IV).

FORTRAN is a popular programming language which is used primarily in scientific and engineering applications. The reason for the continued popularity of FORTRAN is that FORTRAN programs are portable and because of the availability of a large number of math and scientific libraries. FORTRAN programs are easy to port because of the wide acceptance of the FORTRAN 77 standard (and the FORTRAN 66 standard before that) and the easy availability of standard FORTRAN compilers on a large variety of machines.

Given the popularity of FORTRAN and the ease of porting FORTRAN programs, why not continue to program in FORTRAN? The problem with FORTRAN is that it is suited primarily for scientific and engineering programming. Although it has been used for a variety of other application domains such as operating systems, compilers and text processing, FORTRAN is not really suited for these domains: its facilities are tuned for writing scientific and engineering programs. In addition, despite its many revisions, FORTRAN 77 does not have all the necessary ingredients of a modern programming language. This is because the original FORTRAN was designed over a quarter century ago and each revision has attempted to keep the flavor of its predecessor version in an effort to remain upward compatible. For example, FORTRAN 77 does not have the *while* loop, a structured multi-way branching facility, structures, or a type definition facility.

C is an excellent alternative to FORTRAN for serious professional programming in almost every type of programming domain including scientific and engineering applications. It is an extremely popular language that was first made popular by the UNIX system which is now a dominating force in the multi-user operating system market (the UNIX system and its utilities are written in C). C has been used in the past primarily by professional programmers and in the universities. But now, it is the language of choice for serious programmers for just about every type of application and on all types of computers: from PCs to mainframes. C is also extremely portable; moreover, many math and scientific libraries are now available and the number of libraries available is growing rapidly.

The de facto C standard until recently was the C language as described in the *C Reference Manual* contained in the book *The C Programming Language* [Kern78]. We shall refer to this definition of C as K&R C. To ensure more compatibility between compilers, an ANSI standard version of C [ANSI88] has been defined. We shall refer to this version as ANSI C or just C. We will use ANSI C as the basis for describing the C language in this book. ANSI C is a superset of K&R C and many compilers now implement ANSI C.

C is normally used in conjunction with a standard library that contains essential and important utility functions such as those for performing input and output. Until recently, these functions were not considered to be part of C. Instead, these and other utility functions were considered to be part of the "C environment" provided by the C compiler or by the operating system. For example, K&R C assumes the presence of the standard C library functions that are normally supplied by the UNIX system C compiler; it does not describe the standard library functions [Kern78]. On the other hand, the standard library functions are specified to be part of ANSI C and they are defined in the ANSI C documentation [ANSI88]. Each ANSI C compiler is expected to provide these functions as part of its standard C library.

1. C COMPILERS & SOFTWARE

Numerous C compilers are now available for the IBM PC and compatibles, and for almost all other types of computer systems. Here is a partial list of some well known C compilers (in alphabetical order):

- Aztec C86 (from Manx)
- C86 Plus (from Computer Innovations)
- DeSmet DC88 (from C Ware)
- High C (from Metaware)
- Lattice C
- Power C
- Let's C (from Mark Williams)
- Microsoft C
- Turbo C (from Borland)

These compilers are reviewed in *PC Magazine*, v7, no. 15 (September 13, 1988).

C compilers are quite inexpensive; their prices range from about twenty US dollars to several hundred US dollars. The Power C compiler can be purchased at the remarkably low price of $19.95. Here is a review of the Power C compiler from *PC Magazine*:

> Power C is an amazingly inexpensive compiler that implements the full ANSI C standard. It features a superior manual and consistently good performance. Power C is great for educational institutions and hobbyists.

Before buying a compiler, evaluate it to see if it meets your needs. The price of the compiler should be only one of the factors in your making a decision about which compiler to buy. Some other factors that you should consider are the quality of the compiler (is it bug free? does it implement full ANSI C?), the quality of the documentation, the compilation speed, the quality of the object code, the tools that come with it (e.g., a debugger and a profiler), product support from the maker of the compiler, and so forth. Look in the latest issues of the popular personal computer magazines for the most recent evaluations of the latest versions of the C compilers.

Countless software tools and packages are available for the C programmer. To find tools that meet your needs, look at some of the advertisements in recent issues of magazines such as *Byte*, *PC Magazine*, *UNIX Review*, and *Dr. Dobb's Journal*. For example, in a recent issue of *Byte*, C libraries for multitasking, scientific programming, screen graphics, and database utilities were all being advertised by a single software company.

2. GOALS OF THIS BOOK

This book can be used as a text book by FORTRAN programmers who want to teach themselves C or in an advanced C programming course for students who already know FORTRAN. It is not a first book on C. This book is not meant for those new to the programming discipline because it assumes that the readers are well versed in the science of programming. Consequently, there is essentially no discussion of the semantics of basic programming concepts such as assignment, expression evaluation, loops, and so forth. The focus of this book is on C programming and not on the C language syntax.

The first chapter familiarizes the reader with the C programming language by showing several FORTRAN programs along with the corresponding C programs. These C programs are explained in detail along with comments about the ways in which C differs from FORTRAN. The first chapter is followed by chapters that discuss the C counterparts of FORTRAN facilities, and C facilities for which there are no FORTRAN counterparts. Then there are chapters that examine important C facilities individually in detail. There is also a chapter that discusses

FORTRAN facilities for which there are no C counterparts.

Each chapter is interlaced with numerous examples because of the author's conviction that learning programming is facilitated by reading and understanding examples. This is no different from other disciplines. For example, we learn good writing techniques by reading the works of good authors. Whenever appropriate, relevant documents, which are listed in the bibliography, are cited in the text (the citations are enclosed within square brackets).

The examples given in this book are real examples or close approximations thereof; they are not just toy examples. They can be used directly or as components of more elaborate programs. All the examples given in this book have been tested. The C examples were tested using the Turbo C and Microsoft C compilers. The source for all the examples given in this book is available in diskette form from Silicon Press. To facilitate use of this diskette, names of the files containing the code for the examples given in this book are specified in the text.

Finally, I am grateful to the anonymous reviewers who made many suggestions for improving the book.

T. D. Brown, Jr.

CHAPTER 1

INTRODUCTION

C is a general-purpose programming language designed especially for writing efficient and portable programs. C was designed by Dennis Ritchie, circa 1972, at the world-famous AT&T Bell Laboratories, which is also where the popular UNIX system was designed. The goal of C was to replace assembly language programming that used to dominate programming at AT&T Bell Laboratories. C has not only surpassed this goal but it has also succeeded far beyond the designer's expectations. C is now used just about everywhere. Its influence extends from academic institutions to software houses and to personal computer users.

C is a compact programming language that offers a large spectrum of advanced programming facilities for program and data structuring. It is a versatile and flexible programming language that can be used for a wide range of application domains – from writing device controllers to writing database systems. C is routinely used for systems programming and in applications where efficiency and portability is important. C programs are easy to port because of the relatively high degree of standardization. To ensure even more compatibility between compilers, an ANSI standard version of C [ANSI88] has been defined.

This book focuses primarily on the facilities specified in ANSI C and those in ANSI FORTRAN 77.

1. GENERAL COMMENTS ABOUT C

A C program consists of declarations and definitions, a function named *main*, plus zero or more other functions. C makes a distinction between declarations and definitions: *declarations* specify identifier types but they do not allocate storage while *definitions* specify identifier types and, at the same time, allocate storage. Using C terminology, FORTRAN declarations would be called definitions.

Like large FORTRAN programs, large C programs are typically kept in several files. Some C files contain only declarations of variables and functions, and constant and type definitions. Such files are called *header* files. Names of header files are, by convention, given the suffix .*h*. Other files may contain C functions and possibly, definitions, and declarations; these files are called *source* files and their names are given the suffix .*c* (many C compilers will refuse to compile a file that does not have the *.c* suffix). Typically, a C source file will contain one or more related functions, and related item definitions and declarations. Some of these items may be used for communication between functions in the same file and/or between functions in other files. Header files are included in source files or in other header files by using the C preprocessor *#include* statement. (The C preprocessor processes a C program before it is compiled by the C compiler; see Chapter 6.) Source files are compiled with the C compiler to produce object files which are linked together with each other and with libraries using the system linker to produce an executable file.

Floating-point computation semantics are of special concern for FORTRAN programmers especially because many FORTRAN programs are computation intensive with a lot of floating-point arithmetic. The ANSI C standardization committee chose to follow the FORTRAN floating-point model for two important reasons:

1. By choosing this model, they would facilitate FORTRAN-to-C program translation efforts, and
2. The ANSI C committee rightfully felt that the designers of the FORTRAN floating-point model, i.e., the FORTRAN standardization committee, had greater experience with floating-point arithmetic than the ANSI C committee, and that it would be prudent to rely on their experience and build upon this experience instead of starting from scratch.

2. A QUICK TOUR OF THE C LANGUAGE

The rest of this chapter is intended to give you a quick tour of the C language. We will write programs for four problems. For each problem, I will show you a FORTRAN program and then an equivalent C program. Because this book is intended for experienced FORTRAN programmers, the FORTRAN programs given in this book will not be explained in detail. These programs are straightforward, and the reader should not have any trouble understanding them. However, each C program is followed by a detailed discussion and a comparison with the corresponding FORTRAN program. The discussion will include comments about differences between C and FORTRAN. The C concepts presented in this section will, of course, be discussed in depth in later chapters.

The best way to get comfortable in a new programming language is to get "hands-on" programming experience. Consequently, you should compile and run the C programs given in this book on your computer. Hands-on programming will not only make you conversant and comfortable with C quickly, but it will also "acclimatize" you to the C programming environment with the minimum of delay.

A word about the notation used in the text. Both FORTRAN and C programs will be shown in typewriter-like font. Conforming to established conventions, we will use upper-case letters for FORTRAN programs and lower-case letters for C programs. Finally, I will use italic font to refer to FORTRAN and C identifiers and constructs in the text.

2.1 COMPUTING ACCRUED INTEREST EXAMPLE

The first problem involves writing a program to compute the interest paid by a bank on money deposited by the customer. Although different banks may pay the same simple interest rate, the "actual" or compound interest paid by them may be different. This is because the interest accumulated is computed and paid by different banks after different time periods. The more frequently the interest is paid, the more total interest you get, because you start getting interest on the interest itself sooner. For example, other things being equal, you will get more total interest from a bank that pays interest daily rather than from a bank that pays interest quarterly or yearly. (Paying the interest on a daily basis is called *daily compounding*.) The total interest paid by a bank can be computed by the formula

$$i = p*((1+r/(100*np))^{np*yrs} - 1)$$

where

- i is the total interest paid,
- p is the principal amount,
- r is the interest rate in percent,
- np is the number of periods in a year when interest is paid, and
- yrs is the number of years the money is kept on deposit.

First, we will take a look at the FORTRAN version of the program to calculate the interest (stored in file *int.for*):

```
C   Interest Calculation Program
        REAL P, R, I
        INTEGER NP, YRS
        WRITE(*, '(A)') '+principal? '
        READ(*, *) P
        WRITE(*, '(A)') '+interest rate? '
        READ(*, *) R
        WRITE(*, '(A)') '+no. of periods per year? '
        READ(*, *) NP
        WRITE(*, '(A)') '+years? '
        READ(*, *) YRS
        I = P*((1+R/(100*NP))**(NP*YRS)-1)
        WRITE(*, 14) I
14      FORMAT('+total interest = ', F10.3)
        END
```

Now, we will take a look at the corresponding C program (stored in file *int.c*):

```
/*The interest calculation program*/
#include <stdio.h>
#include <math.h>
main(void)
{
    float p, r, i;
    int np, yrs;

    printf("principal?");
    scanf("%f", &p);
    printf("interest rate?");
    scanf("%f", &r);
    printf("no. of periods per year?");
    scanf("%d", &np);
    printf("years?");
    scanf("%d", &yrs);
    i = p*(pow(1+r/(100.0*np), (double) np*yrs)-1);
    printf("total interest = %g\n", i);
}
```

Let us examine the above C program in detail. Lines 2 and 3 (beginning with the character #) are C preprocessor statements. As mentioned earlier, before a C program is compiled, it is processed by the C preprocessor. Although the C preprocessor is not logically part of the C compiler, for all practical purposes it is considered to be an integral part of every C compiler. The C preprocessor is typically used for things such as file inclusion, and constant and macro definitions. The two *#include* instructions in the above C program are used to include the standard header files named *stdio.h* and *math.h* which respectively contain the declarations of the C standard input and output functions, and the declarations of the math functions. Functions, like variables, should be declared before they are used.

Unlike in FORTRAN, in C input and output facilities are not built into the language but, instead, they are part of the standard C library. C also does not have an exponentiation operator. Instead, exponentiation is performed by calling the C math library function *pow*.

Continuing our discussion of the C program, note that the definition of function *main* which begins on line 4. Each C program must contain the distinguished function *main* because the execution of a C program begins by executing this distinguished function. The fact that this *main* function does not have any parameters is specified by the *void* type (line 4). Values for the parameters, if any, of a *main* function are supplied as command-line arguments. Note that in K&R C, a function that does not take any arguments is specified without the *void* type, e.g., as

```
main()
{
    ...
}
```

Each function returns a value of the type specified before the function name. In case of *main*, programmers typically omit specifying the type in which case, by default, the result type of *main* becomes *int* (integer).

The body of each C function, e.g., the *main* function, begins with the left curly brace (line 5) and is terminated by the right curly brace (last line of the program). On the other hand, the body of a FORTRAN main program begins with the first statement (or the *PROGRAM* statement) and that of a FORTRAN subprogram with the second statement. The body of a FORTRAN main program or a FORTRAN subprogram is terminated by the *END* statement.

The first two lines within the body of function *main* (lines 6 and 7) are variable definition statements which define identifiers p, r, and i to be variables of type *float* (single precision) and identifiers *np* and *yrs* to be of type *int* (integer). As mentioned earlier, C makes a distinction between declarations and definitions: *declarations* specify identifier types but they do not allocate storage while *definitions* specify identifier types and, at the same time, they also allocate storage. Other languages do not make this distinction.

All declarations and definitions within a C function must appear before any executable statements. FORTRAN has a similar requirement.

After the variable definitions, there are four pairs of *printf* (output) and *scanf* (input) statements. To be precise, these statements are actually calls to the standard library functions *scanf* and *printf*. These functions are used to read from standard input and to write to standard output. (Functions *fscanf* and *fprintf* are used to read from and to write to arbitrary files.) The functionality of these functions is similar to that of the FORTRAN *READ* and *WRITE* statements.

In FORTRAN, string constants (called literals in C) are enclosed within single quotes. There is no distinction between characters and strings except that a character is a string of length one. In C, string literals are enclosed within double quotes while character literals are enclosed within single quotes. A string is a sequence of (non-null) characters that is terminated by the null character (which is denoted as \0). In case of string literals, the null character is automatically inserted by the compiler. But in other cases, the null character must be explicitly appended at the end of the character sequence by the programmer.

One ramification of providing library functions for input and output instead of statements is that the compiler cannot determine, at compile time, mismatches between the items to be read or printed and the corresponding format items. Moreover, the format items must be explicitly supplied because otherwise the compiler cannot perform the appropriate conversions. As a result, in C there is no counterpart of the list-directed input/output facility of FORTRAN.

Each of the above *printf* function calls has only one argument: the string to be printed. In general, the *printf* function can take a variable number of arguments. The first argument specifies the text to be printed and contains place holders for the other arguments that are all to be printed. The place holders also specify the formats to be used when printing the arguments. The first argument of the *printf* function is called the "format" string.

The *scanf* statement is the input counterpart of the *printf* statement. Each of the *scanf* statements used in the above program has two arguments. The first argument in each of these *scanf* statements specifies that the value to be read is either a floating-point value (*%f*) or an integer value (*%d*), and the second argument gives the address (memory location) of the variable where the value read is to be stored. (Note that the ampersand operator "*&*" extracts the address of its operand.)

Unlike in FORTRAN, in C memory locations (addresses) of variables, which are to be assigned input values, must be given to the input function *scanf*. This is another important difference between the FORTRAN *READ* statement and the C input function *scanf*. It arises not because *scanf* is implemented as a library function but because C does not support passing arguments "by reference" as in FORTRAN. In a FORTRAN function or subroutine*, the parameters (dummy arguments) become synonyms for the arguments (actual arguments). Consequently, arguments can be used to send values to a function or to a subroutine and parameters (along with the function result) can be used to send values back to the caller of the function or the subroutine. In C, arguments are passed "by value", i.e., the parameters are set to the values of the corresponding arguments, but the reverse does not happen upon completion of the function. To return results to the caller, either the function returns a result or the function changes the contents of the memory locations (addresses) passed as arguments to the function; the latter technique is used to simulate the FORTRAN semantics of passing arguments "by reference".

Each executable C statement must be terminated by a semicolon unless it ends with a right curly brace. Unlike FORTRAN, C is a free format language. Multiple C statements can be put on one line. And a C statement can span multiple lines; continuation marks are not required. C statements can be in any column (including columns 1 through 6).

After the four *printf* and *scanf* statement pairs, the C program has an assignment statement. Note that this statement contains a cast, i.e., type conversion, which is

---

*   The C counterpart of the FORTRAN subroutine is a function that does not return a value, i.e., a *void* function.

denoted as (*double*): the integer expression *np*yrs* is converted to a double precision value to match the requirements (specification) of function *pow*.

The assignment statement is followed by another *printf* statement that prints a message and the value of variable *i*. In this statement, format item *%g* specifies that argument *i* is to be printed in "g" format. Depending upon the value to be printed, the "g" format instructs the *printf* function to select the most appropriate of the floating-point or the scientific formats to print the corresponding argument.

Assignment is an operator in C and not a statement as in FORTRAN. The value of an assignment expression is the value assigned to the variable on the left of the assignment operator. If the value of an expression is not used, then it is simply discarded. Appending a semicolon to any expression transforms the expression into a statement. This allows an assignment expression to be written like a statement, for example,

```
i = p*(pow(1+r/(100*np), np*yrs)-1);
```

2.1.1 DIFFERENCES BETWEEN THE FORTRAN & C PROGRAMS. The differences between the two interest calculation programs are now summarized:

1. An important difference between the two programs is that the FORTRAN program must obey the strict format rules of FORTRAN. C programs do not have such constraints because C is a free format language. For example, in FORTRAN comments must begin in column 1 with the character C, statements must begin in column 7 or after, continuation marks must be placed in column 6, characters past column 72 are ignored, lines can be only 80 characters long and so forth. C statements and comments can begin and end in any column and there is no need for continuation marks.

    Each C statement must end with a semicolon but it can span multiple lines; multiple statements can also be given on one line. From the point of view of the C compiler, it does not matter whether or not a C statement fits on a single line or it spans several lines. If a statement, such as the one in the *then* part of a C *if* statement, is an extra long one, then it can be simply continued on one or more lines.

2. A FORTRAN comment occupies the whole line by itself while a C comment (which begins with a "/*" and ends with a "*/") can be given any where a space is allowed in a C program and it can span multiple lines.

3. Although we have declared all the variables in the FORTRAN program, this is not required by FORTRAN. The types of variables that are not explicitly declared are determined according to the rules specified by FORTRAN. C, on the other hand, requires all variables to be declared or defined before they are referenced. At a first glance, requiring explicit declarations may seem to be unnecessary and inconvenient from the

programmer's perspective. A careful study of this requirement can lead you to the following conclusion reached by many well-known computer scientists: explicit declarations can improve program readability and documentation, and can help the programmer detect errors at an early stage of the program's life cycle. Almost all new languages now require variables to be explicitly declared before they are used.

4.   Input/output facilities are built into FORTRAN but not into C. In case of C, these facilities are provided by means of library functions that must be provided by every C compiler. Consequently, as discussed earlier, C compilers cannot, at compile time, type-check the arguments to be read or printed with the corresponding format items and C cannot support list-directed input/output.

5.   C does not support the FORTRAN semantics of argument passing. In a FORTRAN subprogram, arguments are passed "by reference" in that the parameters become synonyms for the corresponding arguments. Consequently, arguments can be used to send values to and return values from a subprogram. In C, arguments are passed "by value", i.e., the parameters are set to the values of the corresponding arguments, but the reverse does not happen upon completion of the function. FORTRAN argument passing semantics are simulated in C by passing pointers to variables, i.e., by passing the addresses of the memory locations where the variables are stored (pointers are discussed in later chapters). As we shall see, this important difference in argument passing semantics has a strong impact on the way C programs are written.

6.   Exponentiation is an operator in FORTRAN but in C it is a standard math library function. The reason why C does not provide an operator is simply a matter of the C design philosophy, according to which, an operator should be in the language only if the corresponding operation can be performed by one machine instruction.

7.   A FORTRAN main program is a program unit that does not begin with a *FUNCTION, SUBROUTINE,* or *BLOCK DATA* statement. It may begin with a *PROGRAM* statement. In C, the main program is a function with the special name *main.* The *main* function is like any other C function.

2.1.2 COMPILING & RUNNING C PROGRAMS. Let us now discuss the execution of the above C program. As mentioned above, the C version of the interest calculation program is stored in the file named *int.c.* By convention, the *.c* suffix is used for names of files containing executable C statements (that is, C code; files containing C code are also called C *source* files). For the purpose of illustration, we shall use a Turbo C compiler (on an MS-DOS system) to compile and link C programs. Note that Microsoft C compiler commands are similar.

File *int.c* is compiled and linked by the Turbo C command *tcc* to produce an executable file *int.exe*:

```
tcc int
```

The Turbo C command *tcc* operates in two phases. First it produces an object code (machine language) translation of the above interest calculation program and stores it in the file *int.obj*. Then this object file is linked together with the input and output functions and the math function *pow* that are used in the calculator program:

The C program can now be executed by simply typing

```
int
```

which causes file *int.exe* to be executed.

Both the Turbo C and Microsoft C compilers also provide interactive menu-based formats for interactively compiling and editing C programs.

2.2 FILE COPY EXAMPLE

The second problem involves writing a program to read input from the keyboard (the standard input), and then print this input on the display (the standard output). By appropriately redirecting the input and the output, this program can also be used to display the contents of a file, store the keyboard input in a file, and copy files.

First, the FORTRAN program (stored in file *c.for*):

```
        CHARACTER*80 LINE
85      READ(*, '(A80)', END=99) LINE
        WRITE(*, 20) LINE
20      FORMAT(1X, A80)
        GOTO 85
99      CONTINUE
        END
```

The FORTRAN program reads input from the standard input, one complete line at a time, and then prints the line on the standard output.

Now, the C program (stored in file *c.c*):

```
#include <stdio.h>
main(void)
{
    int c;

    while ((c = getchar()) != EOF)
        putchar(c);
}
```

The C program reads characters, one at a time, from the standard input, i.e., the keyboard, and writes them on the standard output, i.e., the display. Lines are not treated especially. Input and output (and files) are streams of characters. An end of a line is not of any special significance; it is simply indicated by the new-line character. C input functions combine the line-feed and carriage-return characters into one character called the new-line character. C output functions do the reverse; that is, they translate a new-line character to the line-feed and carriage-return characters.

The above C program contains one definition, that of variable *c*, which is declared to be an integer, and one executable statement, the *while* loop. The *while* loop expression consists of a call to the input function *getchar*, which reads a character from the standard input. This character is stored in the integer variable *c*. The loop (and consequently the program) terminates when function *getchar* returns -1. *EOF* is a symbolic constant defined as -1 in the header file *stdio.h* by using the preprocessor *#define* statement.

Notice that *EOF* is written in upper case while everything else is written in lower case. Traditionally, C programs are written predominantly using lower-case letters. Upper-case letters are used for preprocessor definitions (as in the case of *EOF*) and sometimes for user-defined type names.

C character variables are essentially integer variables. Character values can be stored in integer variables and non-negative integers in character variables. Variables used for storing characters read by functions such as *getchar* are defined as integer variables because these functions return a -1 to indicate the end of file. (Note that -1 does not correspond to the representation of any valid character.)

The body of the *while* loop consists of a single statement: a call to the function *putchar* which prints its argument on the display. Functions *getchar* and *putchar* are usually, but not always, implemented as macros for efficiency: minimization of execution time. Macros are defined using the C preprocessor (discussed in Chapter 6).

Suppose the above C program is stored in file *c.c*. Then this program can be compiled and linked using the Turbo C compiler command

```
tcc c
```

which produce file *c.exe*, the executable version of *c.c*.

The executable program *c.exe* can be invoked in several different ways to make it do different things. For example, invoking it simply as

```
c
```

causes it to read characters from the terminal and print them on the display.

If input is redirected from a file, then program *c.exe* can be used to display a file on the display:

```
c  <source-file
```

If output is redirected to a file, then *c.exe* can be used to store characters, typed at the keyboard, in a file:

```
c  >target-file
```

If both input and output are redirected, then program *c.exe* can be used to copy files:

```
c  <source-file  >target-file
```

2.2.1 DIFFERENCES BETWEEN THE FORTRAN & C PROGRAMS. We will now examine the main differences between the FORTRAN and C versions of the file copy program:

1. The lack of a *while* loop facility in FORTRAN forces the use of *GOTO* statements which the computer science community by and large now considers to be bad for programming. FORTRAN *GOTO* labels are integer constants and they must be given in columns 1 through 5. C labels must be identifiers (which is more mnemonic); there is no restriction on the columns in which they can appear (being a free-format language, C does not favor any specific column).

2. Assignment is a statement in FORTRAN but it is an operator in C. Consequently, in C you are likely to see many expressions, such as the *while* loop expression, which contain the assignment operator. This allows C programmers to write compact code; assignment is performed as a side effect during expression evaluation.

3. FORTRAN input lines can be only 80 characters long; there is no such restriction on C input lines.

4. FORTRAN input/output is line-oriented while C input/output is character-oriented. For example, the FORTRAN program gets its input on a line-by-line basis while the C program gets its input on a character-by-character basis. C treats the new-line character just like any other character. Typically, C programs expect their input to be a character stream.

5. In FORTRAN, the end-of-file is detected by using the *END* option of the *READ* statement. In C, by convention, input functions return *EOF* (-1) when they encounter an end of file. Consequently, detecting an end of file is simply a matter of checking if the value returned by an input function signals an end of file. For example, *getchar* indicates that it has reached the end of file by returning -1.

6. By default, in FORTRAN the *READ* and *WRITE* statements operate on a new line. In C, reading and writing resumes at the point where it was left

off.

7. C does not have FORTRAN's notion of carriage control. Carriage control characters are used to alter the behavior of the *WRITE* statement. In C, the printing behavior is altered by printing appropriate characters such as the new-line and form-feed characters.

2.3 POCKET CALCULATOR EXAMPLE

The third problem involves writing a calculator program to perform addition (+), subtraction (-), multiplication (*), and division (/). The calculator displays the "running" total in its internal accumulator after each of the above operations. Entering the character "c" clears the internal accumulator. The calculator is "turned off" by typing the control-break character which terminates the program.

Here is the FORTRAN version of the calculator program (stored in file *calc.for*):

```
C calculator program
      REAL RESULT, OPD
      CHARACTER OPR
85    RESULT = 0
      WRITE(*, 10) RESULT
10    FORMAT(3X, G10.4/)
      READ(*, '(F10.0)') RESULT
99    READ(*, '(A1)') OPR
      IF (OPR .EQ. 'c') GOTO 85
      IF (OPR .NE. '+' .AND. OPR .NE. '-'
     C      .AND. OPR .NE. '*' .AND. OPR .NE. '/') THEN
          WRITE(*, *) '***ERROR***'
          STOP
      END IF
      READ(*, *) OPD
      IF (OPR .EQ. '+') THEN
          RESULT = RESULT + OPD
      ELSE IF (OPR .EQ. '-') THEN
          RESULT = RESULT - OPD
      ELSE IF (OPR .EQ. '*') THEN
          RESULT = RESULT * OPD
      ELSE IF (OPR .EQ. '/') THEN
          RESULT = RESULT / OPD
      END IF
      WRITE(*, 10) RESULT
      GOTO 99
      END
```

The FORTRAN program expects each item of input on a new line because of the line-oriented nature of its input (and output) facilities. C input/output is not line-oriented. As a result, the C program given below does not impose this restriction. Multiple items can be given on the same line.

Now here is the C version of the calculator program (stored in file *calc.c*):

```
/*calculator program*/

#include <stdio.h>
#include <ctype.h>
main(void)
{
    float result = 0, opd;
    int opr;

    printf(" %g\n", result);
    scanf("%f", &result);  /*first operand*/
    for (;;) {
        while (isspace(opr = getchar()))
            ;
        if (opr == 'c') {
            printf(" %g\n", result = 0);
            scanf("%f", &result);  /*first operand*/
            continue;
        }
        if (opr != '+' && opr != '-' &&
                    opr != '*' && opr != '/') {
            printf("***error***\n");
            exit(1);
        }
        scanf("%f", &opd);
        switch (opr) {
            case '+': result += opd; break;
            case '-': result -= opd; break;
            case '*': result *= opd; break;
            case '/': result /= opd;
        }
        printf(" %g\n", result);
    }
}
```

As mentioned earlier, C comments begin with the characters "/*" and are terminated by the characters "*/". Comments cannot be nested. But they can be given anywhere in a C program where a blank space is allowed. This does not mean that you should start inserting comments in the middle of expressions as in

```
a = a /*and now multiply by 5*/ * 5;
```

If comments are not given and placed judiciously, then they will not facilitate program understanding; instead, they are quite likely to do the exact opposite.

Variables *result* and *opd* are declared to be floating-point variables; *float* is initialized to 0.0. Unlike in the FORTRAN program, variable *opr* in the C program is declared as integer (*int*) even though it supposed to hold a single character designating the calculator operation. This is because *getchar*, the input function which is used to get the next character, returns a -1 to signal the end of file.

The program starts off by printing the value of *result* (using the *g* format). Initially, the value of *result* is zero. This is followed by the new-line character denoted by the two-character sequence "\n". The backslash character is called the *escape* character. Printing the new-line character causes the cursor (or the print position) to skip to the beginning of the next line. Then the value of the first operand is read into the variable *result*.

The calculator program then enters an infinite loop which is specified by a *for* statement of the form

```
for (;;)
{
    ...
}
```

Next comes the *while* loop which reads characters until it encounters a "non-space" character. Here is how the execution of the *while* loop proceeds. The *while* expression is evaluated first. Evaluation means calling function *getchar* to read a character from the standard input (the keyboard is the default standard input) and assigning it to the variable *opr*. The result of this assignment is the final value of *opr* which is then passed to function *isspace* (whose declaration is contained in the header file *ctype.h*). This function returns true (1) if its argument is one of the following characters: a blank, a tab, a carriage-return, a new-line, or a form-feed character. Otherwise, it returns false (0). If the *while* expression is true, then the null statement (denoted by the semicolon), which is the body of this loop, is executed; otherwise, the loop terminates. By giving an expression that always evaluates to true, the *while* loop can be used to specify an infinite loop.

Loops with null bodies are a peculiar C phenomenon. You will often encounter such loops in C programs. The loop expression does all the work while the loop body does nothing.

Following the *while* loop is an *if* statement which checks to see if the operator stored in *opr* is the calculator clear command *c*. Operator "= =" is the C comparison operator. Be careful when using it because a common mistake is to leave out one of the "=" characters. A single "=" character denotes the assignment operator, and assignment, unlike in most other languages, is allowed in C expressions. The result of an assignment expression is the value assigned to the lefthand variable. Consequently, assigning a non-zero value means that the assignment expression will evaluate to true and assigning a zero value means that the assignment expression will evaluate to false.

We have used curly braces for the *then* parts of the *if* statements so that we can give multiple statements in the *then* parts. C allows you to combine several statements into one logical statement by enclosing the statements within curly braces. This allows the use of several statements in places where the C syntax requires a single statement. For example, the C syntax specifies that the *then* and *else* parts of an *if* statement must be single statements.

An assignment expression is used within the *printf* statement given inside the body of the *if* statement. It resets the variable *result* to zero which is the value then printed. The *continue* statement causes the rest of the statements in the loop to be skipped and the next iteration to be started. The semantics of the C *continue* statement are quite different from the semantics of the FORTRAN *CONTINUE* statement, which is a kind of place holder or a null statement.

After the *if* statement comes another *if* statement which checks to see whether or not *opr* contains a valid calculator operator. In case the user of this calculator program types an invalid operator, the program is terminated by calling function *exit*. By convention, function *exit* is called with the value zero to indicate successful program completion; abnormal or failed program termination is indicated by calling *exit* with the value one. Function *exit* can also be called with other values to indicate other program completion states. The *exit* function should be used to terminate a program if program termination information is to be passed back to the program creator, i.e., the parent program (see your compiler reference manual for more details).

As in FORTRAN, nested *if* statements can be used in C for multi-way branching. But C also provides another control structure, called the *switch* statement, for multi-way branching. In many cases, the *switch* statement can be easier to read and more efficient to implement than nested *if* statements. The *switch* statement evaluates its expression and jumps to the alternative with a *case* label whose value matches that of the *switch* expression. Statements following the *case* label are then executed.

Let us now consider the *switch* statement in this program. The *switch* expression consists of just the variable *opr*. Depending upon the value of this variable, the value of *opr* is added to, subtracted from, multiplied with, or divided into that of variable *result*, and the result of this operation is then stored in *result*.

The first statement after each *case* label is an assignment statement. In addition to the conventional assignment facility, C provides several other types of assignment facilities. For example, the operator "+ =" increments its left operand by the value of its left operand; the statement

```
result += opd;
```

is equivalent to the assignment

```
result = result + opd;
```

After each of the first three assignment statements inside the *switch* statement is the *break* statement, which is used to exit from the *switch* statement. In the absence of the *break* statement, control will flow from one *switch* alternative to the next. Some programmers often exploit this "feature" for "efficiency" reasons, e.g., to avoid duplicating code. However, allowing control to flow from one alternative to another is dangerous because it can lead to errors. For example, statements can be changed in a *switch* alternative without realizing that control also flows to the changed alternative from the previous alternative.

The *switch* statement also has a default alternative (with the *case* label *default*). This alternative covers the cases for which a label has not been explicitly specified.

2.3.1 DIFFERENCES BETWEEN THE FORTRAN & C PROGRAMS. There are some important differences between the FORTRAN and C versions of the calculator program:

1. Because of line-oriented nature of FORTRAN input and output, the FORTRAN program is written so that each input item is entered on a new line. Because C input and output are character-oriented, the C program does not have these restrictions. Even though the input to the C calculator program may be given on one line, the program can read the input in appropriate amounts. Unlike the FORTRAN version, the C version does not have to digest the input one whole line at a time.

2. The lack of a facility in FORTRAN equivalent to the C *while* loop forces the use of *GOTO* statements in FORTRAN programs.

3. The absence of a general *switch* statement† in FORTRAN forces the use of the nested *IF* statements which are typically less efficient (because each logical expression may have to be evaluated) than a *switch* statement.

4. The C notation for the relational operators such as $<$, $>$, $<=$, etc. is more in math style than the FORTRAN notation *.LT.*, *.GT.*, and *.LE.*.

2.4 DOUBLE-WORD CHECKER EXAMPLE

A common mistake that people make when entering text into a computer file with a text editor is to enter the same word twice in a row. Double words can be on the same line as in

```
Alice in in Wonderland
```

or on different lines as in

```
Alice in
in Wonderland
```

---

† The computed *GOTO* statement can be used to simulate a limited form of the *switch* statement.

The problem is to write a program that finds occurrences of such double words in a file and then prints the numbers of the lines containing (at least one of) the double words.

For our purposes, we will define a word to be any continuous sequence of non-space characters on the same line. Although this definition simplifies writing of the double-word checker, it also means that we will not be able to detect double word occurrences such as the one illustrated in the following sentence:

She brought great news news.

This is because, according to our definition of a word, the second "news" will not be a word by itself; instead, it will be part of the word "news." because there is no blank space preceding the period. Refinements of the double-word checker program to cover the above situation and other situations that are not handled by it are left as an exercise for the reader.

Here is the FORTRAN version of the double-word checker (stored in file *double.for*):

```
        CHARACTER LAST*16, NEXT*16, LINE*80
        INTEGER LNO, N
        COMMON LNO, LINE, N
C LNO=line number, N=position to start looking for a new word
C from (N=0 means read a new line)
        LOGICAL WORD
        LNO = 0
        N = 0
        LAST = '                '
95      IF (.NOT. WORD(NEXT)) GOTO 99
        IF (LAST .EQ. NEXT) WRITE(*, 21)LAST, LNO
21      FORMAT(1X, 'double word **', A, '** on line ', I4)
        LAST = NEXT
        GOTO 95
99      STOP
        END
```

The above program uses function *WORD* (stored in file *word.for*):

```
C Put the next word from the input stream in W.
C As the function result, return .FALSE. upon
C encountering end of file; otherwise return .TRUE.
C
        LOGICAL FUNCTION WORD(W)
        CHARACTER W*16, LINE*80
        INTEGER LNO, N, I, J
        COMMON LNO, LINE, N
C
        W = '                        '
C
C  read new line if necessary
C
30      IF (N .EQ. 0) THEN
            READ(*, 31, END=201) LINE
31          FORMAT(A)
            LNO = LNO + 1
            N = 1
        END IF
C
C skip leading blanks
C
        DO 202 I = N, 80
            IF (LINE(I:I) .NE. ' ') GOTO 203
202     CONTINUE
        N = 0
        GOTO 30
C
C put the next word in W, I points to first non blank
C
203     J = 1
        DO  205 N = I, 80
            IF (LINE(N:N) .EQ. ' ') GOTO 206
            W(J:J) = LINE(N:N)
            J = J + 1
205     CONTINUE
        N = 0
206     WORD = .TRUE.
        RETURN
201     WORD = .FALSE.
        END
```

Function *WORD* is used to get the next word from the input and to determine the end of file.

Like FORTRAN, C also supports independent compilation. To illustrate independent compilation in C, we will store the C version of the double-word checker program in three separate files. The first file, *double.h*, contains the declarations used in the other files. The other two files, *double.c* and *word.c*, contain code for the *main* function which does the double word comparison, and for function *word* which gets words from the input file (it disassembles the input file into a stream of words).

Each file containing C program text is equivalent to a *module* (program unit in FORTRAN). (We shall use the terms file, module, and program unit interchangeably.) Breaking up a program into small modules is important for writing large programs. First, information local to a module can be hidden from other modules. Second, it is easier to update and maintain small modules rather than large ones. Third, compiling (or editing) a small module is faster than compiling (or editing) a large module. Finally, after a program has been modified, only the modified modules and other modules that depend upon the modified modules need to be recompiled (this process can be automated by using a program called *make* which is available from several software companies such as Borland and Microsoft).

Here are the contents of the declarations file *double.h*:

```
#include <stdio.h>
#define WL 80

extern int line_no;
int word(char []);
```

The second line of the above file is the C preprocessor *#define* statement which defines *WL* to be a symbolic constant with the value 80. Like the FORTRAN program, the C program assumes that the maximum length of the words in the file is not more than 80 characters, which is quite a reasonable assumption.

The third line in the above header file is a blank line. Blank lines are often inserted in C programs to increase program readability. The C compiler ignores blank lines just as it ignores comments.

The fourth line is a C declaration which declares an external integer (*extern int*) variable, named *line_no*, that will be used for inter-function communication (like the *COMMON* variables in the FORTRAN program). These functions can be in the same file or in different files. If this global (external) variable is to be used only for intra-file inter-function communication, then it should be declared as a *static* variable. The scope of global static variables is restricted to the file containing them which prevents functions in other files from accessing these variables.

Storage for an external variable can be allocated only in one module. The definition of an external variable is just like its declaration, but it does not use the keyword *extern*. An external variable definition must be given outside a function body.

Several files can reference the same external variable, by giving identical declarations (one file must contain a matching definition for the external variable), allowing functions to communicate with each other by reading and updating these external variables. External variables represent one of the two primary mechanisms in C for inter-function communication, the other being function arguments (see Chapter 4 for more details).

The fifth line in the header file *double.h* is the declaration of the function *word* which is called by function *main* to get the next word. This declaration is called a *prototype* function declaration because it gives all the syntactic and type information necessary to call the function. This function prototype specifies that function *word* takes as an argument a character array and returns an integer value.

Function prototypes should always be given before calling a function because they provide the compiler with information that it can use to detect errors. If a function prototype is not given then, by default, the function result (return) type is assumed to be *int* (integer). Moreover, without prototype declarations the compiler will not be able to check whether or not the function is called with the right number of arguments and whether or not the argument types match the parameter types. Please remember, as mentioned earlier, that the terminology used in FORTRAN for arguments is "actual arguments" and for parameters it is "dummy arguments".

Prototype declarations are new to C; they were introduced by ANSI C and are not present in K&R C. In K&R C, function *word* would be declared as

```
int word();
```

Here is the *main* function (stored in file *double.c*):

```
#include <string.h>
#include "double.h"
int line_no = 1;

main(void)
{
   char next[WL+1], last[WL+1];

   last[0] = '\0';
   while ((word(next)) != EOF) {
     if (strcmp(next, last) == 0)
        printf("double word **%s** on line %d\n",
                                        last, line_no);
     strcpy(last, next);
   }
}
```

We have seen the *#include* statement several times before. However, this is the first time that it has been used to include a user-defined header file. The file to be included, *double.h*, is enclosed in double quotes instead of angle brackets as done in the earlier *#include* instructions. The only difference between the use of angle brackets and double quotes is that for file names enclosed in double quotes, the C preprocessor looks in the current directory before looking in the standard places where it expects to find the files. Of course, in either case (whether angle brackets or double quotes are used), if an absolute path name is specified, as in

```
#include "\pc\driver\laser.h"
```

then there is no need to search directories.

A file inclusion capability is important for program modularization. Common declarations and definitions can be kept in one file and program modules that need the declarations can include the declarations file. This way the declarations do not need to be typed again for every module. Including a declarations file also ensures that every module has exactly the same declarations thus avoiding possible errors.

The next line is the definition of the external variable *line_no* (note the absence of the keyword *extern*) whose declaration we saw in the header file *double.h*. A definition can be preceded by a declaration although the declaration will be redundant and not really necessary. However, a redundant declaration can help ensure that the definition matches the declaration which is what is given in the other modules. In our case, the declaration of *line_no* was included by including the header file *double.h*. This file was included for the other declarations contained in it which are required by *main*.

After the definition of *line_no* is the definition of function *main*. The variable definition statement inside function *main* defines two character arrays, *next* and *last*, both of size *WL* + 1. Array subscripts in C start with 0, so each of the above arrays will have subscripts ranging from 0 to *WL*. These arrays will be used to hold words from the input document.

Array elements are referenced using square bracket to specify the subscripts. For example, the statement

```
last[0] = '\0';
```

assigns the null character to the first element of array *last* which, according to the convention used in C, means that *last* contains the null string. Note that one pair of square brackets must be given for each subscript.

After the above assignment statement, there is a *while* loop whose expression contains a call to the user-defined function *word*. Function *word* stores the next word from the input file in the array argument *next* and it then returns the word length as its result. If *word* encounters the end of file, then it returns the constant *EOF* (-1).

The body of the *while* loop contains calls to two string functions, *strcmp* and *strcpy*, which are part of the standard C library. *strcmp* compares its two arguments, which must be strings, and returns -1, 0 or 1 depending upon whether its first argument is lexically less than, equal to, or greater than its second argument. *strcpy* copies its second argument to the first one.

One final comment about the above *main* function: function *printf* prints a string (its first argument), the string variable *last*, and the integer variable *line_no*. The latter two are printed according to the format specifiers embedded within the first argument. Strings are printed using the format specifier "%s" and integers are printed using the format specifier "%d". The format specifiers also implicitly specify the position where the corresponding arguments will be printed within the string specified as the first argument.

Here is the definition of function *word* (stored in *word.c*):

```c
#include <ctype.h>
#include "double.h"

int word(char s[]) /*returns length of s, or EOF*/
{
  int c, i = 0;

  while ((c = getchar()) != EOF) {
    if (isspace(c)) {
      if (c == '\n') line_no++;
      if (i == 0)  /*skip leading white space*/
        continue;
      s[i] = '\0';  /*end of word*/
      return i-1;
    }
    s[i++] = c;
  }
  return EOF;
}
```

word is a user-defined function that returns, as its result, an integer value. The function result is specified with the *return* statement. An interesting thing to note is that the new-line character '\n' can be compared with any other character because '\n' is just another character, e.g., like 'a'. The effect of the *continue* statement in the *while* loop is to skip execution of the remaining part of the current loop iteration and go on to the next iteration. Notice the use of the increment expression "*i*++" to specify the subscript of array *s*. The value of this expression is the original value of variable *i*, but as a side effect of evaluating this expression, the value of *i* is incremented by one.

These two C files (*double.c* and *word.c*) were compiled separately by using the following Turbo C command

```
tcc -edouble double word
```

The executable file produced by this command is named *double.exe*. Note that the executable file name was explicitly specified with the -e option of the *tcc* command. See your compiler reference manual for details on how to compile C files, and then link together the object files produced to construct an executable file.

2.4.1 DIFFERENCES BETWEEN THE FORTRAN & C PROGRAMS. Once again, we will now examine the differences between the two versions of the double-word checker program:

1. The C program is smaller and easier to read than the FORTRAN program. Most people familiar with both these languages will agree with this assessment.

2. Because of the line-oriented input in FORTRAN, function *WORD* has to read input one whole line at a time; this line is then parsed into words. On the other hand, the C program reads input one character at a time and it does so in chunks corresponding to complete words. This makes the C function *word* simpler than the corresponding FORTRAN function *WORD*.

3. The FORTRAN program can only read files with lines that are of the defined length which is 80 characters in this example. This is because input in FORTRAN is line-oriented and because we have to specify, in advance, the size of the array that will hold the line. The C program is more flexible; it can handle input lines of any length.

4. Unlike FORTRAN, C does not have a logical type; instead, it treats zero as false and non-zero values as true.

5. The common declarations used in the C *main* and *word* functions are kept in the header file *double.h* and included in the files containing references to and definitions of these functions by means of the C preprocessor *#include* statement. In case of the FORTRAN program, the common declarations, i.e., the *COMMON* statement and the matching type declarations, cannot be kept in a common header file because there is no file inclusion facility in standard FORTRAN. Declarations common to multiple functions must be given explicitly in the functions where they are needed. Compared to the use of a file inclusion facility, this increases the probability of inadvertently giving different declarations in different files.

6. In FORTRAN, the *COMMON* statement is used to specify variables that will be shared by multiple functions and to save the values of function variables across function calls (the latter can also be done with the *SAVE* statement). In C, *extern* variables are used as shared variables, *static* variables defined outside a function body are used as variables that will be shared only by functions in the same file, and *static* variables declared inside a function body are used to retain values across function calls.

7. FORTRAN has two types of subprograms: subroutines and functions. C has only functions. Functions that do not return values are like FORTRAN subroutines except that no special keyword (like the keyword *CALL* in FORTRAN) is needed when calling them.

8. FORTRAN arguments are passed by reference while C arguments are passed by value. Passing arguments by reference in C is simulated by

passing pointers to arguments instead of passing the arguments themselves.

9.   The function result in a FORTRAN program is specified by assigning the result to the function identifier. In C, the function result is specified using the *return* statement. Note that the semantics of the *return* statement are quite different in the two languages.

10. FORTRAN strings are of fixed length while C strings are of varying length. C strings are terminated by the null character \0. In C, a string is cleared by simply setting it to the null string which is done by setting the first character to the null character. In FORTRAN, we had to clear the string by setting the whole string to blanks (this can be quite expensive for large strings; alternatively, we can keep track of the string length explicitly by using an extra variable for each string variable, which can then be set to 0 to set a string to the null string).

     As a consequence of the way FORTRAN treats strings, it was simpler to just print all the 16 characters in variable *LAST* to indicate the double word even though it would have been nicer to not print the trailing banks in *LAST*.

11. Elements of C strings are referenced like array elements; in fact, C strings are character arrays. FORTRAN string elements are referenced using the substring notation.

12. Strings can be compared with the *.EQ.* operator in FORTRAN, but in C the library function *strcmp* must be used.

13. The lack of the right control structures in FORTRAN forces programmers to use *GOTO* statements which are rarely seen in C programs.

14. In C, square brackets are used to specify array subscripts while in FORTRAN parentheses are used. One pair of square brackets must be used for each C subscript, while all the FORTRAN subscripts must be enclosed in one pair of parentheses. The C syntax makes it easy to differentiate between an array element reference and a function call.

3. FINAL COMMENTS

The objective of this chapter was to familiarize you with the C programming style and show you some differences between FORTRAN and C. The differences in the two languages lead to different programming styles for the two languages. In terms of functionality, it is important to note that you can write the same programs in FORTRAN that you can write with C and vice versa. FORTRAN is mainly appropriate for scientific programming. C is suitable for writing programs for a wide variety of application domains including scientific programming. In this chapter, we looked at C from a high-level perspective. In subsequent chapters, we will take a closer look at C.

4. EXERCISES

1. Compile, link, and execute the example C programs on your computer.

2. What will be the effect of nesting comments in a C program?

3. Suppose you erroneously use the assignment operator "=" instead of the equality operator "==" as in the following *if* statement:

```
if (opr = '+')
    ...
```

   Explain the consequences of your mistake.

4. Rewrite the C version of the calculator program in which the *if* statement and the nested *switch* statement are combined into just one *switch* statement that uses the *default* alternative (see Chapter 3 for more details about the *switch* statement).

5. The double-word checker does not catch double phrases such as

```
that book that book
```

   Extend the double-word program to handle two-word phrases. Note that you only have to modify the *main* function (and not function *word*).

CHAPTER 2

FORTRAN FACILITIES PRESENT IN C
& VICE VERSA

C and FORTRAN have many facilities in common, for example, integer and floating-point types, and assignment and loop statements. However, there are many C facilities that are not present in FORTRAN and vice versa. The goal of this chapter is to primarily discuss FORTRAN facilities that can be found in C and vice versa: the corresponding facilities may match exactly, or they may just be similar. The next chapter will discuss C facilities for which there are no FORTRAN counterparts, and a later chapter will discuss FORTRAN facilities for which there are no C counterparts. Other chapters will discuss in detail some of the important facilities provided by the C language.

When discussing and comparing C and FORTRAN facilities, C syntax and semantics will also be discussed. This will be done informally, but in sufficient detail to enable you to use the C constructs without any problem. If you need to refer to the complete and formal syntax of C, for example, if you are writing a program to analyze or compile C programs, then please refer to the ANSI C Reference Manual [ANSI88].

1. GENERAL COMMENTS ABOUT C

A C program consists of declarations, a function named *main*, plus zero or more other functions. A large C program is typically kept in several files. Some files may just contain declarations in which case they are called *header* files. Names of header files are, by convention, given the suffix *.h*. Other files may contain C functions and possibly, definitions, and declarations; these files are called *source* files and their names must have the suffix *.c*. Typically, a C source file will contain one or more related functions, and related item definitions and declarations. Some of these items may be used for communication between functions in the same file or between functions in other files. Header files normally contain declarations that will be used by multiple functions. Header files are included in source files or other header files by using the C preprocessor *#include* statement. To produce an executable file, source files are compiled with the C compiler to produce object files which are then linked together with each other and with libraries using the system linker.

2. BASICS OF C

2.1 C CHARACTER SET

C specifies a source character set and an execution character set. The basic source and execution character sets consist of the

1. Upper-case and lower-case letters. Unlike FORTRAN, C is case sensitive which means that C distinguishes between upper- and lower-case characters. For example, C does not consider the names *max* and *MAX* to be identical.

2. Ten decimal digits.

3. Graphic characters: ! " # % & ' ( ) * + , - . / : ; < = > ? [\ ] ^ _ { | } ~

4. Formatting characters: space, horizontal-tab, and form-feed characters.

In addition, the source character set must include some way of specifying new lines; the basic execution character set must include the null character (denoted as \0) and control characters representing alert (terminal bell), a backspace, a carriage return and a new line.

Space, tab and new-line characters along with comments are called the *white space* characters.

Note that C character set is different from the ASCII character set.

2.2 COMMENTS

C comments begin with the character pair "/*" and are terminated with the character pair "*/". Comments can be inserted wherever a blank is allowed. Unlike in FORTRAN, comments in C can be embedded within a single- or a multi-line statement, and a single comment can itself span multiple lines. This is why C comments must be terminated explicitly. Here is an example of a multi-line comment:

```
/*-------------------------------

   FORTRAN to C Conversion Program

-------------------------------*/
```

If you forget to terminate a comment in a C program, then the C compiler will treat the rest of the program until the next character pair "*/", if any, as comments. Note that nested comments are not allowed in C.

2.3 STATEMENT TERMINATION, MULTIPLE STATEMENTS PER LINE & LONG STATEMENTS

All C statements, except executable statements that end with a right curly brace (i.e., compound statements), must be terminated with a semicolon. C is a free-format language, that is, multiple statements can be placed on a single line or a single statement can span several lines. Unlike in FORTRAN, line boundaries in C do not make any difference.

2.4 IDENTIFIERS (NAMES)

Identifiers (names) are used as symbolic references for items such as constants, memory locations, types, and functions. A C identifier (symbolic name in FORTRAN) is a sequence of letters, digits, or underscores that begins with a letter or an underscore. By convention, identifiers that begin with an underscore are used only in system programs and not in application programs.

C identifiers can be of any length. However, in case of internal identifiers only the first 31 characters are considered to be significant; in case of external identifiers (such as function names) only the first six characters are considered significant. Of course an implementation may choose to be more flexible than this and allow identifiers with longer significant lengths. In case of FORTRAN identifiers, only the first 6 characters are considered significant.

2.5 VARIABLES

As in FORTRAN, C variables are identifiers that are associated with memory locations. There is not much difference in the use of variables in the two languages except that the type of a C variable must be explicitly specified in a definition or declaration before it can be used.

2.6 KEYWORDS

As in FORTRAN, some C identifiers are reserved words that cannot be used as user-defined identifiers in programs. Here is a list of the C keywords [ANSI88]:

auto	double	int	struct
break	else	long	switch
case	enum	register	typedef
char	extern	return	union
const	float	short	unsigned
continue	for	signed	void
default	goto	sizeof	volatile
do	if	static	while

In addition to the keywords, some identifiers are reserved for use by the C implementation. Identifiers defined or declared in the standard header files, which are supplied by every C compiler, and names beginning with an underscore and followed by another underscore or an upper-case letter are reserved words. Identifiers defined in the standard header files denote pre-defined constant names, type names, function names, and macro names. Here are some specific examples: *NULL, EOF*, and *strcmp*.

2.7 CONSTANTS (LITERALS)

Like FORTRAN, C provides facilities for specifying integer, single and double precision floating-point, and string (character in FORTRAN) constants (literals). In addition, C provides facilities for specifying single character, long (double precision) integer, unsigned integers (unsigned integers are discussed later), and extra large double precision floating-point constants. However, because C does not have pre-defined logical and complex data types, it does not provide facilities for specifying logical and complex constants.

Octal and hexadecimal notation can be used for specifying integer constants in C. Octal constants are specified with a leading 0 (as in 022), and hexadecimal constants are specified with a leading 0x or 0X as in (0x5A). In case of hexadecimal constants, the digits 10 to 15 are denoted by the letters A to E (or a to e).

The letter l (or L) at the end of an integer constant specifies that it is a long integer (or simply long) constant. And the letter u (or U) at the end of an integer constant specifies that it is an unsigned integer. By default, floating-point constants are interpreted as double precision constants. Single precision floating-point constants are specified by using the suffix f (or F) and extra large double precision constants are specified using the suffix l (or L). The letter e (or E) is used to specify the exponent of floating-point constants written in the scientific notation, for example, 3.198e2 (i.e., 319.8).

C string constants are specified by enclosing a sequence of characters within double quotes. Note that when specifying string (character) constants in FORTRAN, single quotes are used instead of double quotes.

FORTRAN does not distinguish between characters and strings. Characters are just strings of length one. C characters are not the same as one-character strings. This is because in C strings are sequences of characters terminated by the null character which is denoted as "\0". For example, the string "a" actually consists of two characters: the letter a and the null character. Note that, by convention, the null character is not counted in the string length.

C also provides a special denotation for some non-printing characters and some characters that have a special role in the C syntax (so that they can be treated like ordinary characters):

\a	(alert)
\b	(backspace)
\\	(backslash)
\r	(carriage return)
\"	(double quote)
\f	(form feed)
\t	(horizontal tab)
\n	(new line)
\0	(null character)
\?	(question mark)
\'	(single quote)
\v	(vertical tab)

The backslash character is used to suppress the special role played by some characters in C. For example, to include the double quote character in a string, the denotation "\"" is used. The alternative denotations of the single and double quote characters with the preceding backslash allow them to be treated as ordinary characters and not as delimiters.

In addition, any arbitrary character can be denoted as "\ddd" where *ddd* stands for one to three octal digits specifying the internal encoding of the character. Also, any arbitrary character can be denoted using the notation "\x*hexadecimal-digits*"; any number of hexadecimal digits may be used. Note that the interpretation of the octal and hexadecimal character sequences is implementation dependent (because C is not tied to the ASCII character set). This notation is used especially for specifying control characters and other non-printing characters. For example, the escape character *esc* is denoted as \033 (provided the compiler uses the same encoding as ASCII for the escape character).

Character constants are denoted by enclosing the specified character in single quotes, for example, *'c'*, *'0'*, *'\n'*, and *'\033'*.

2.8 SYMBOLIC CONSTANTS

Like FORTRAN, C provides facilities for giving symbolic names to constants. This facility is actually provided by the C preprocessor. Constants are given symbolic names by using the *#define* instruction which has the form

```
#define  name  constant
```

The # character must be the first non-white-space character on a line. Typically, the # character is placed in column one. The *#define* instruction shown here is a special case of the more general form allowed by the C preprocessor.

Here are some examples of constant definitions:

```
#define MAX 132
#define WORD_SIZE 4
#define TRUE  1
#define FALSE 0
#define NULL  0
#define EOF (-1)
```

Symbolic names can enhance program readability and can make it easier to modify and maintain programs. For example, if the value of a symbolic constant is to be changed, then only the constant definition will need to be changed and not all uses of the constant.

2.9 VARIABLE DECLARATIONS/DEFINITIONS

In FORTRAN, simple variables do not have to be explicitly declared. Array variables have to be declared but their types do not have to be explicitly specified.

In these cases, the first letter of a variable is used to determine the variable type according to rules prespecified in FORTRAN or as specified explicitly with the *IMPLICIT* statement.

Being able to deduce a variable's type from its name enhances program readability (provided the *IMPLICIT* statement has not been used to override the prespecified rules). However, deducing variable types from their names is not appropriate or practical for a language like C which allows the user to declare an arbitrary number of new types.

Because simple variables need not be explicitly declared in FORTRAN, variables whose names are misspelled are treated as new variables. Consequently, errors due to misspelled variable names may not be detected by the FORTRAN compiler. In C, all variables must be defined (or at least declared) before they can be used. As a result, misspelled variable names are immediately detected by C compilers because both the variables name as used and as given in variable definitions (or declarations) must match exactly.

C variable declarations are of the form

type   declarator-list ;

where *declarator-list* contains the items being defined (declared). We will not formally explain the declarator syntax; instead, it will be illustrated by means of examples given throughout the book. Here are some examples of variable definitions:

```
int i;
float f, g = 0.0;
char line[128];
employee e;
```

These definitions specify

- *i* to be an *int* (integer) variable,
- *f* and *g* to be *float* (floating-point) variables with *g*, initialized to 0.0,
- *line* to be a *char* (character) array of length 128, and
- *e* to be a variable of the user-defined type *employee*.

Variables can be initialized, as illustrated by the initialization of *g*, in their definitions. Type *employee* used in the last definition is not a pre-defined type provided by C, but instead it is a type defined by the user with the *typedef* facility. We shall discuss user-defined types in more detail later.

3. FUNDAMENTAL TYPES

C has all the types that FORTRAN has except the complex type. Numerous operators and library functions are provided for manipulating objects of these types. Strings are implemented as character arrays and C provides numerous library functions for manipulating strings. In addition, C provides, as components of the standard libraries, numerous functions for manipulating these objects (see the Appendix).

Types in C are classified into two categories: *fundamental* (or *basic*) types provided by the language, and *derived* types which are built from the fundamental types. C supports the following fundamental types: character, integer, floating-point, and enumeration types (see Chapter 3). Character and integer types are collectively called the *integral* types; integral and floating-point types are collectively called the *arithmetic* types. Derived types will be discussed in the next section.

Unlike FORTRAN, C does not have a Boolean (*LOGICAL*) type. C treats a non-zero integer value as true and zero as false. Consequently, logical variables are typically declared to be integer variables.

3.1 CHARACTER TYPE

The C character type is denoted by the identifier *char*. Here are some example definitions of character variables:

```
char a;
char c, delim = ':';
```

C provides many functions for classifying character values; for example, there are functions to determine if a character is alphabetic, numeric, alphanumeric, or printable. Functions for character conversion, such as those for converting characters from one case to another, are also provided. Details of these functions are given in the Appendix.

Mixing integers and characters is a common C paradigm. In fact, C programmers treat *char* variables as very small (8-bit) integers. Integers, such as negative integers, that are not valid encodings of characters should generally not be stored in *char* variables; otherwise, the result may be undefined. If a character variable occasionally has to store an integer that does not correspond to a valid character encoding, or if a function that normally returns characters occasionally returns such an integer, then it should be defined as an integer and not as a *char*. For example, function *getchar* that normally returns the next character from the standard input, returns *EOF* (-1) to indicate the end of file. Consequently, *getchar* is defined to be of the integer type *int*.

3.2 INTEGER TYPES

C has three integer types which are denoted as *int*, *short*, and *long*. Types *short* (or *short int*) and *long* (or *long int*) are variations of type *int* which offer less and more precision, respectively, than type *int*. Due to the difference in precision, *short* and *long* variables, respectively, require less and more storage than variables of type *int*. Type *int* is usually mapped to the natural word size of the machine. Some compilers may treat *short* as a synonym for *int* offering no saving of storage or difference in precision. Similarly, other compilers may treat *long* as a synonym for *int*. However, most compilers do provide at least two flavors of integers, that is, they do not treat both *short* and *long* to be synonyms of type *int*. On IBM PCs and compatible computers, C compilers typically treat *short* as a synonym for *int* implementing both *short* and *int* using one word of memory. But type *long* is treated differently from type *int* and is implemented using two words.

Integers of the types discussed above are called *signed* integers. If the representation of an integer (the way an integer is stored in a computer word) is to be manipulated as a bit pattern, then the *unsigned* integer type should be used. In the case of *unsigned* integers the sign bit is not treated as a special bit. Because of this, unsigned integers can also be used to hold larger positive integers.

Here are some examples of integer variable definitions and function declarations:

```
int i;
short a = 0, b = -1;
long p;
int getchar(void), scanf(const char *, ...);
```

The last line is a declaration because it does not cause any storage to be allocated. It declares *getchar* to be a parameterless function that returns an integer result and *scanf* to be a function whose first argument is a constant pointer to a string. This argument may be followed by a variable number of arguments and *scanf* returns an integer result.

3.3 FLOATING POINT TYPES

C has two floating-point types: a single precision floating-point and a double precision floating-point. These types are denoted as *float* and *double*. In ANSI C, *float* is a full-fledged type as one would expect. But this is not the case in K&R C because all *float* values are converted to *double* before performing any operation (and, if necessary, converted back to *float* after the operation). In K&R C, the main reason for using *float* is to save storage; however, the use of *float* does slow program execution due to the conversions that are required when operating on *float* values.

Here are some examples of floating-point variable definitions:

```
float f;
double a, b;
```

3.4 CONVERSION BETWEEN FUNDAMENTAL & POINTER TYPES

Character values can be used as integer values and vice versa. Integral values are automatically converted to floating-point and vice versa. C uses truncation to convert floating-point values to integers; for example, 2.75 and 2.25 both yield 2 when they are converted to integers.

In C, an expression of a fundamental or a pointer type can be converted to any fundamental or pointer type by *casting* (converting) the expression to the desired type. Casts have the form

(*new-type*) *expression*

As an example, suppose that *a* is a floating-point variable and *p* is an integer-pointer variable. (Pointers are discussed in detail in Chapters 2 and 5.) The following expressions

```
(int) (a*a)
(char *) p
```

yield the integer equivalent of *a*a* and a character pointer equal in value to the integer pointer *p*, respectively. Notice that in the first case, casting involves calling a function to do the conversion while in the second case only the pointer type is changed and no computation is actually performed to do the conversion.

4. DERIVED TYPES

Derived types are types constructed using fundamental types and previously defined derived types. Types that can be derived are arrays, structures, unions, and pointers. Except for arrays, FORTRAN has no counterparts for the other derived types. We shall discuss arrays in the following section and the other derived types in Chapter 3.

4.1 ARRAYS

Arrays in FORTRAN and C are conceptually quite similar, but there are differences. For example, the lower bounds of C arrays must be zero while those of FORTRAN arrays can be any values as long as they are less than or equal to the corresponding upper bound. Unlike in FORTRAN, the storage order of the elements of an array is not specified by C. But perhaps the most important difference between FORTRAN and C arrays is that in FORTRAN arrays are a full-fledged type while in C arrays are really a convenient mechanism for accessing storage referred to by pointers. As a result, C compilers do not perform subscript checking. Lack of subscript checking prevents many errors from being detected at an early stage in a program's life cycle. From the compiler's viewpoint, the bounds of an array are significant only in that they allow the compiler to determine the amount of storage that must be allocated for the array.

As in the case of FORTRAN arrays, the bounds of a C array must be specified when defining an array. However, when an array with explicitly specified initial element values is defined, then the size of the first dimension need not be given; the missing array dimension size is automatically computed by the C compiler by counting the number of initial values.

As an example of C arrays, consider the following array definitions:

```
int a[10], b[25][5], c[5][5][5];
```

a, *b*, and *c* are defined to be one-, two-, and three-dimensional arrays, respectively. Notice that square brackets are used to specify the array dimensions. In FORTRAN, one pair of parentheses is used to specify all the array dimensions. In C, on the other hand, a pair of square brackets must be used for specifying each dimension of an array. This is because an *n*-dimensional array in C is thought of as an array with (*n*-1)-dimensional elements.

The C notation for referencing array elements is similar to the FORTRAN notation with two exceptions: square brackets are used (instead of parentheses) and each subscript must be enclosed in square brackets as in

```
a[i]
b[i]
b[i][j]
c[i][j][k]
```

Dynamic arrays, that is, arrays whose dimensions are specified by arbitrary expressions, can be implemented in C. Dynamic arrays are made possible by the special relationship between arrays and pointers which we shall discuss in Chapter 5. Dynamic arrays allow C programmers to define arrays of exactly the size needed for the program. In FORTRAN, array sizes are static and the programmer must declare arrays that are large enough to handle all possible cases even though, in most cases, smaller arrays may be sufficient. Use of larger than necessary arrays wastes storage, which can be a critical resource for some applications.

To illustrate the use of arrays in C, we will write a program that reads characters from the standard input and counts the number of times the various letters occur in the input. No distinction will be made between lower- and upper-case letters.

Array *ct* will be used to store the letter counts: element $f[c\text{-}'a']$ will store the number of times letter *c* appears in the input. (All C arrays begin with the subscript zero. Had it been possible to specify alternative first subscripts, as in FORTRAN, for example, that the first subscript of *ct* be the integer encoding of the letter "a", then the number of times letter *c* appears in the input would have been stored in element *ct*[*c*].)

Here is the C program that counts the number of times letters appear in its input (stored in file *freq.c*):

```
#include <stdio.h>
#include <ctype.h>

#define NO_LET 26

int ct[NO_LET];   /*external variables are */
                  /*initialized to zero, by*/
                  /*default*/
main(void)
{
    int c, i;

    while ((c = getchar()) != EOF)
        if (isalpha(c)) {
            c = tolower(c);   /*convert to lower*/
            ct[c-'a']++;
        }
    for (i=0; i < NO_LET; i++)
        printf("%c count = %d\n",i+'a',ct[i]);
}
```

As before, you can use input redirection to count the number of times letters appear in any file.

As another example of arrays, here is a function that adds two integer vectors (one-dimensional arrays) and puts their result in a third:

```
void vadd(int a[], int b[], int c[], int n)
{
    int i;

    for (i = 0; i < n; i++)
        c[i] = b[i] + a[i];
}
```

The *void* (empty) type specifies that function *vadd* does not return any value; that is, *vadd* is for all practical purposes a subroutine. Notice that array dimensions are not specified in the declarations of parameters *a*, *b*, and *c*. Function *vadd* assumes that each of the three arrays has at least *n* elements. When calling a function with array arguments, it is often necessary to pass their sizes as additional arguments.

We will conclude this section on arrays with one final example. With a sorted array, the *binary search* technique can be used to locate the index of an array element with a specific value. The binary search technique first examines the middle element of the array to see if it is equal to the search value. If yes, then the search is complete. Otherwise, if the search value is less than the middle element, then the upper portion of the array is "binary searched"; if the search value is more than the middle element, then the bottom portion of the array is "binary searched" (assuming that the array elements are sorted in increasing order). On the average, binary search is much faster than sequential search; this difference becomes more noticeable as the array size increases.

Here is function *search* that implements binary search (stored in file *search.c*):

```
/*search sorted array a for value x; return*/
/*k such that a[k]==x; otherwise, return -1*/

int search(int a[], int n, int x)
{
    int l = 0, u = n-1, k;

    while (l <= u)
        if (a[k = (l+u)/2] == x)
            return k;
        else if (a[k]<x)
            l = k+1;
        else
            u = k-1;
    return -1;
}
```

Notice the use of the assignment operator in the array subscript expression, within the *if* expression, to compute the midpoint k of the array. Had the assignment to k been done before the *if* statement, as would be done in languages like FORTRAN in which assignment is not an operator, then the *while* loop in the above program would have been written as

```
while (l <= u) {
    k = (l+u)/2;
    if (a[k] == x)
        return k;
    else if (a[k]<x)
        l = k+1;
    else
        u = k-1;
}
```

4.1.1 ARRAYS ARE NOT FULL-FLEDGED OBJECTS. C arrays are not full-fledged objects like other derived types such as pointers and structures (both are discussed later). For example, array assignment is not allowed while pointer and structure assignment is allowed.

4.2 STRINGS

Unlike FORTRAN, C does not have a built-in string type. Instead, in C, strings are implemented as character arrays. By convention, strings are terminated by the null character '\0'. This is a very important convention that no C programmer can afford to forget. Strings must be terminated with the null character; otherwise, none of the library string functions will work properly. C compilers also follow this convention; they automatically add the terminating null character at the end of each string literal.

As an example illustrating string manipulation, consider the following code that is used to read, from standard input, all the characters up to the next blank and store them in the character array *word*:

```
int c, i = 0;
char word[MAX+1];

while ((c = getchar()) != EOF)
    word[i++] = c;
word[i] = '\0';
```

Notice that the string is terminated explicitly by storing the null character at the end of the array. (Statement "*word*[*i*++] = *c*;" is equivalent to the statement "*word*[*i*] = *c*;" followed by the statement "*i*=*i*+*1*;".)

Because strings are not a built-in type in C, there are no built-in facilities to manipulate strings. For example, there are no built-in operators for string assignment, string concatenation, and string comparison. But as part of the standard library, C compilers provide many functions for manipulating strings. For example, function *strcpy* does string assignment, function *strcat* does string concatenation, and function *strcmp* does string comparison. String functions are classified into the following categories: copy, concatenation, comparison, length, and searching. Details of the string functions are given in the Appendix.

One of the string functions provided by the C compiler is *strlen* which determines the length of a string. Had this function not been provided, then it could have been easily written as

```
int strlen(char s[])
{
    int i = 0;
    while (s[i++] != '\0')
        ;
    return i-1;
}
```

Function *strlen* simply counts the number of characters up to, but not including, the terminating null character. The importance of the terminating null character at the end of a string cannot be emphasized too much. In the absence of this character, the above loop will go through all of memory, examining every byte, until it finds a null character or until it references an illegal address which will cause the program to terminate.

Array names are (constant) pointers to the beginning of the storage allocated for the array. Therefore, in this example, array *s* could also have been declared as a character pointer. The declaration of the library function *strlen*, which is given in the Appendix, declares *s* as the character pointer

```
char *s;
```

and not as an array as declared in the above program. Because of the special relationship between arrays and pointers (see Chapter 5), these two declarations are equivalent: C arrays are essentially "syntactic convenience" for pointers. Often strings are manipulated using pointers instead of arrays.

C provides many string manipulation functions (see the Appendix). And new functions can be easily implemented. As an example, consider function *left* which extracts the left substring of the specified length from the specified source string (stored in file *left.c*):

```
#include <stdlib.h> /*decl. of exit*/
#include <stdio.h>
#include <string.h>
void left(char d[], char s[], int n)
            /*set d to the leftmost n*/
            /*characters of s          */
{
    if (n < 0 ) {
        fprintf(stderr, "error, n is negative\n");
        exit(1);
    }
    if (n > strlen(s))
        n = strlen(s);
    strncpy(d, s, n);
    d[n] = '\0';
}
```

Function *left* expects three arguments: the destination string *d* where the extracted substring will be stored, the source string *s*, and the substring length *n*. For example, to extract and store the leftmost 4 characters of string *y* in string *a*, function *left* is called as

```
left(a, y, 4);
```

The algorithm implemented by *left* is simple: after ensuring that *n* in not negative, *left* checks to see if *n* is greater than the length of *s* by calling the string length function *strlen*. If *n* is greater, then it is set to the length of *s*. *left* then copies the first *n* characters of *s* to *d* by calling function *strlen*. A terminating null character is then added at the end of *d*.

Function *left* returns a *void* (empty) value as it result. This is how subroutines are written in C. Consequently, a call to this function cannot be used in an expression; the call must be made into a statement by appending a semicolon (it becomes like a FORTRAN subroutine call except that it is not preceded by a keyword like *CALL*).

If *left* is to be used in expressions, we can easily modify it to return the left substring as its value (stored in *leftr.c*). For This time we will allocate the destination string *d* in *left* itself instead of passing it as an argument:

```
#include <stdio.h> /*also contains defn. of NULL*/
#include <stdlib.h> /*decls. of exit & malloc*/
#include <string.h>

char *left(char s[], int n)
    /*return pointer to string that contains*/
    /*the leftmost n characters of s*/
{
    char *d;

    if (n < 0 ) {
        fprintf(stderr, "error, n is negative\n");
        exit(1);
    }
    if (n > strlen(s))
        n = strlen(s);

    if ((d = malloc(n+1)) == NULL) {
        fprintf(stderr, "not enough heap storage\n");
        exit(1);
    }
    strncpy(d, s, n);
    d[n]= '\0';
    return d;
}
```

Modifications to the original version of *left* were straightforward: the header of *left* was modified appropriately, *d* was declared and storage allocated for it in *left*, and the address of *d* was returned at the end of the function.

d is declared as a character pointer and not as an array so that storage for it can be allocated on the heap (by calling function *malloc*). Had *d* been declared as a local array variable, then it would be allocated on the stack and its storage would disappear upon the completion of the function. Storage allocated in the heap does not automatically go away after a function completes. In fact, it is the programmer's responsibility to explicitly deallocate such storage, when it is no longer needed, by calling function *free*. Storage for objects pointed to by a pointer variable is typically allocated on the heap but the pointer variable itself may be allocated on the stack. Note that pointers (which FORTRAN does not have) and heap storage go together.

This example makes use of the special relationship between arrays and pointers, i.e., although *d* is declared as a character pointer it is also used as an array (to set the last element of *d* to the null character). Arrays and pointers can be used interchangeably (see Chapter 5) but unlike pointer variables, array names are constants and they cannot be assigned new values. As an example illustrating this difference, consider the following code:

```
char s[MAX+1], t[MAX+1];
int n;
   ...
t = left(s, n);
```

The above assignment is invalid because a new value cannot be assigned to the array name *t*. However, the string returned by *left* can be explicitly copied into the existing elements of array *t* by using the string copy function:

```
strcpy(t, left(s, n));
```

The assignment shown above would have been valid had *t* been defined as a character pointer.

4.2.1 IN CORE (MEMORY) CONVERSIONS USING STRINGS. Using function *sprintf*, formatted output can be written to a string instead of a file. Similarly, using function *sscanf*, formatted input can be read from a string instead of an input file. In fact, these two functions can be used for performing arbitrary type conversions: values are written to a string with one format and then read from the string using another format. Conversions can also be accomplished by writing to a file in one format and then reading from the file in another format. However, conversions using files will be slower than those done using strings because file accesses are much slower than string accesses.

5. OPERATORS & EXPRESSIONS

5.1 OPERATORS

C is a language rich in operators. C has unary, binary, and even ternary operators. There are many more operators in C than in FORTRAN and there are several operators for which there are no direct counterparts in FORTRAN. Examples of such operators are the conditional expression operator, the many compound assignment operators, the *sizeof* operator, and the increment/decrement operators. In addition there are several operators associated with the derived types structures, unions, and pointers which are not supported by FORTRAN.

Unlike FORTRAN, C does not provide any operators for manipulating strings. Instead, as mentioned before, the C standard library contains a large number of functions for manipulating strings. C does not have an exponentiation operator. Instead, the math library function *pow* is used for exponentiation.

Like FORTRAN, C does not provide an integer division operator which would converts its operands to integers before doing the division. The general division operator can be used for integer division, but if its operands are not integers, then they must be explicitly converted to integers before the division is performed. For example, in the expression

```
(int)  a  /  (int)  b
```

the floating-point variables *a* and *b* are explicitly cast (converted) to integers (type *int*) using the cast operator so that integer division is performed. The cast operator is discussed later.

C treats array subscripts (specified with square brackets) and function calls (specified with parentheses) as operators. Like other operators, the subscript and function call operators have precedence and associativity rules. In FORTRAN, as in most other languages, array subscripts and function calls are not considered to be operators; instead, they are considered to be part of the array or function name.

Unlike the corresponding FORTRAN logical operators, C logical operators || (or) and && (and) are conditional, that is, their second operands are evaluated only if it is necessary.

Assignment is an operator in C but not in FORTRAN. Like other operators, the assignment operator can be used in expressions. Indeed, such use is common practice when writing C programs. Besides assigning a value to a variable, the assignment operator produces a result: the value assigned to the variable.

5.1.1 USUAL ARITHMETIC CONVERSION RULES. C arithmetic operators automatically convert their operands to values of appropriate types, according to what are called the "usual arithmetic conversion" rules, before operating on them. These conversion rules are listed below in the order in which they are performed:

1. If one operand is of type *long double*, then the second operand is converted to *long double*.

2. If one operand is of type *double*, then the second operand is converted to *double*.

3. If one operand is of type *float*, then the second operand is converted to *float*.

4. Operands of type *char* and *short int* are converted to *int*. Then, if appropriate, the following conversions are performed:

   a. If one operand type is of type *unsigned long int*, then the second operand is converted to *unsigned long int*.
   b. Else, if one operand is of type *long int* and the second operand is of type *unsigned int*, then the second operand is converted to *long int* (in case the second operand type does not fit in a *long int*, then both are converted to *unsigned long int*).
   c. Else, if one operand is of type *long int*, then the second operand is converted to *long int*.
   d. Else, if one operand is of type *unsigned int*, then the second operand is converted to *unsigned int*.

e.   Else, both operands must be of type *int*.

We shall now discuss the C operators. Remember that the "usual arithmetic conversion" rules are always applied by the arithmetic operators and these conversion rules play a part in determining the result type.

5.1.2 POSTFIX OPERATORS.

Operation	Operator	Operands	Result Type	Notes
function call	( )	function name & argument list		
subscript	[ ]	array name & integral subscript		
direct selection	.	structure or union name, & the component name		
indirect selection	->	pointer to structure or union & the component name		
increment	++	scalar	operand type	increments operand; result is initial operand value
decrement	--	scalar	operand type	decrements operand; result is initial operand value

Here are two examples each of the above operators:

```
getchar()
strlen(s)

a[5]
line[i][j+1]

d.month
e.name

pd->month
pe->name

a++
a = c++;

a[i--]
f(j--)
```

In most languages, as in FORTRAN, function call and subscripting are not considered to be operators. Because C assigns the highest precedence to these operators (and to the structure and union component selection operators), they and their arguments can be thought of, as in FORTRAN, to be part of the associated name. However, when two of these operators appear adjacent to each other, then it becomes necessary to think of them as operators and use operator associativity rules to parse the expression.

FORTRAN does not have operators for selecting structure and union components because it does not support the structure and union data structures. It also does not have operators for incrementing or decrementing variables, but these can be trivially implemented using assignment.

5.1.3 *UNARY OPERATORS*.

Operation	Operator	Operands	Result Type	Notes
dereferencing	*	pointer to any type but *void*	base type	
address of	&	*register* variables and bit fields not allowed.	pointer to the variable's type	
subtraction	–	arithmetic	arithmetic	
logical not	!	arithmetic or pointer	*int*	
one's complement	~	integral	integral*	
increment	++	scalar	scalar	increments the operand; result is the final operand value
decrement	––	scalar	scalar	decrements the operand; result is the final operand value
size of	`sizeof`	expression or type name	integer	use as *sizeof(a)*

Note the following equivalence

`*(&a)` $\equiv$ `a`

where a is any variable.

The *address of* operator is used to extract the address of a variable, i.e., its starting location in memory. This operator is used frequently especially for passing the address of a variable as a function argument to simulate passing arguments "by reference." We shall discuss this in detail later.

Systems programs often require the ability to manipulate bits of a word. As an example, suppose that the last four bits in the status word of a device such as printer are to be cleared (set to zero). Unlike FORTRAN, C provides facilities for bit manipulation. The *bitwise complement* operator comes in handy for manipulating bits of a word. Consider the following assignment which clears all but the last four bits of the *unsigned* variable *status*:

```
status = status & ~15;
```

& is the *bitwise and* operator that "ands" the corresponding pairs of bits of its two operands and for each pair it returns 1 if both the bits are 1; otherwise, it returns 0.

The integer constant 15 is stored as the binary constant

```
1111
```

with leading zeros to fill the machine word. Its complement, i.e., ~15, is stored as the binary constant that has leading 1s and is followed by four 0 bits at the end.

The above assignment could also have been written using an octal constant as

```
status = status & ~017;
```

We could have also written the above assignment without using the bitwise complement operator as (assuming that *unsigned* variables are implemented as 16 bit words)

```
status = status & 177760;
```

The bitwise complement operator saves us the trouble of determining the number with a bit pattern such that all of its bits are ones with the exception of the last four which are zeros. Writing this number explicitly, i.e., without using the one's complement operator, requires knowing the size of the computer's word. Clearing the bits of *status* without using the complement operator will make the code unportable between machines that have different word sizes.

The C increment and the decrement operators add one to and subtract one from a variable, respectively. For example, the statement

```
++p;
```

is equivalent to

```
p = p + 1;
```

If *p* is a pointer variable of type *T*, then adding a one to it implies that *p* is to be increased by the size of *T*. Using the cast operator (i.e., the type conversion operator which is discussed in the next section) and the *sizeof* operator, adding one to *p* is equivalent to the assignment

```
p = (T *) ((int) p + sizeof(T));
```

where T * specifies the type "pointer to T". Notice the ease with which pointers can be converted to integers and integers converted to pointers.

FORTRAN does not have operators to manipulate pointers (& and *) because it does support the notion of pointers. It does not have a *sizeof* operator which is typically used for dynamic storage allocation in conjunction with pointers. And as mentioned before, it does not have the increment or decrement operators.

5.1.4 CAST OPERATOR.

Operation	Operator	Operand	Result Type	Notes
cast	(*T*)	scalar	type T	e.g.,(*int*) *a*

The cast operator is used for explicitly specifying conversions between the arithmetic types, between the pointer types, and between pointers and integers. FORTRAN does not have a cast operator but it does provide functions for converting between its arithmetic types. Moreover, it does not have any pointer types.

5.1.5 MULTIPLICATION/DIVISION OPERATORS.

Operation	Operator	Operands	Result Type
multiplication	*	arithmetic	arithmetic*
division	/	arithmetic	arithmetic*
remainder	%	integral	integral*

FORTRAN does not have the remainder operator but the remainder can be easily computed by using integer division.

---

* The integral or arithmetic type of an operator result conforms to the result type as specified by the "usual arithmetic conversion" rules.

5.1.6 ADDITION/SUBTRACTION OPERATORS.

Operation	Operator	Operands	Result Type	Notes
addition	+	arithmetic or pointer types	arithmetic* or pointer type	in case of a pointer, the integral operand is multiplied by the size of the pointer's base type before the addition
subtraction	–	arithmetic or pointer types	arithmetic* or pointer type	in case of a pointer and an integral operand, the integral operand is multiplied by the size of the pointer's base type before the subtraction; when one pointer is subtracted from another, the result is divided by the size of the pointer's base type

5.1.7 SHIFTING BITS OPERATORS.

Operation	Operator	Operands	Result Type	Notes
left shift	<<	integral	same as left operand	0-fill for vacated bits
right shift	>>	integral	same as left operand	0-fill for vacated bits if left operand is *unsigned*; otherwise, sign bit is propagated

As mentioned, FORTRAN does not have any bit manipulation operators. It was not designed for systems programming and therefore no facilities were provided for bit manipulation. In fact, FORTRAN's goal was to provide a high-level interface that hides bits from the user.

As an illustration of the use of bit shifting, consider the following expression which evaluates to 1 if bit i of the variable *status* is on (i.e., it has the value 1); otherwise, it returns 0:

---

*   The integral or arithmetic type of an operator result conforms to the result type as specified by the "usual arithmetic conversion" rules.

```
status & (i << 1)
```

5.1.8 COMPARISON OPERATORS.

Operation	Operator	Operands	Result Type
less than	<	arithmetic or pointer	int (0 or 1)
greater than	>	arithmetic or pointer	int (0 or 1)
less than or equal to	<=	arithmetic or pointer	int (0 or 1)
greater than or equal to	>=	arithmetic or pointer	int (0 or 1)
equality	==	arithmetic or pointer	int (0 or 1)
inequality	!=	arithmetic or pointer	int (0 or 1)

5.1.9 BITWISE AND and OR OPERATORS.

Operation	Operator	Operands	Result Type
bitwise and	&	integral	integral*
bitwise exclusive or	^	integral	integral*
bitwise inclusive or	|	integral	integral*

5.1.10 LOGICAL AND and OR OPERATORS.

Operation	Operator	Operands	Result Type
logical and	&&	arithmetic or pointer	int
logical or	||	arithmetic or pointer	int

Unlike the corresponding FORTRAN logical operators, C logical operators ||
(or) and && (and) are conditional, that is, their second operands are evaluated
only if it is necessary. For example, if the first operand of the && operator is
false, then the second operand will not be evaluated. And if the first operand of
the || operator is true, then the second operand will not be evaluated.

Conditional evaluation of FORTRAN logical operators used to be discussed as
an optimization technique. But formally defining the semantics of logical
operators to include conditional evaluation, as in C, can be a programming asset.
As an example, consider the following program fragment (a loop with a null
body) that searches an n-element array a for a value x:

```
for (i=0; i<n && a[i] != x; i++)
    ;
```

---

* The integral or arithmetic type of an operator result conforms to the result type as specified
  by the "usual arithmetic conversion" rules.

The second operand of the loop termination expression

```
i<n && a[i] != x
```

will not be evaluated if i is equal or greater than n. Accessing $a[n]$ would be semantically illegal since the largest subscript of a is n-1 (C arrays start with the subscript 0). Because C does not do subscript checking, accessing array elements using invalid subscripts can cause program errors which sometimes results in strange program behavior.

5.1.11 CONDITIONAL EXPRESSION OPERATOR. The conditional expression operator, which has three operands, has the form

$$b \ ? \ e_t \ : \ e_f$$

The result of the above expression is e_t if b is non-zero; otherwise, it is e_f. Expression b must be of an arithmetic type. The other two operands must be of the same type or of types that are automatically convertible to the same type.

The following conditional expression yields 0 if a is negative and a otherwise:

```
a < 0 ? 0 : a
```

There is no equivalent of the conditional expression operator in FORTRAN. In fact an expression such as the one shown above cannot be written directly. In FORTRAN, an intermediate variable, say *AA*, will have to be set to the appropriate value

```
IF (A .LT. 0) THEN
     AA = 0
ELSE
     AA = A
END IF
```

and this variable must then be used in an expression.

5.1.12 ASSIGNMENT (SIMPLE & COMPOUND) OPERATORS. The simple assignment operator = is used as follows:

var = exp

Both variable *var* and expression *exp* must be of arithmetic types, or of identical pointer or structure types. In case of arithmetic types, the value of *exp* is converted to the type of *var*. The effect of the above assignment is to assign the value of *exp* to variable *var*; this value is also the result of the assignment expression.

In addition to the simple assignment operator, C also has several compound assignment operators. These operators allow assignment expressions of the form *var = var op exp*

to be abbreviated as

var op= exp

where *op=* is a compound assignment operator. Here is a list of the C compound assignment operators: + =, - =, *=, / =, % =, > > =, < < =, & =, ^=, and | =.

Compound assignment expressions are not only shorter, but they can be easier to understand and they may help the compiler to generate more efficient code.

For example, the expression

```
x[a>0?a:-a] = x[a>0?a:-a] + i
```

can be better written as

```
x[a>0?a:-a] += i
```

Note that an equivalent assignment may be written in FORTRAN as

```
IF (A .GT. 0) THEN
    TMP = A
ELSE
    TMP = -A
END IF
X(TMP) = X(TMP) + 1
```

5.1.13 COMBINING EXPRESSIONS OPERATOR. Suppose a programmer needs to write multiple expressions in places where the language syntax allows only one expression, for example, only a single expression each is allowed for controlling the *while* loop or the *if* statement. In C, this can be done easily with the comma operator. Two expressions e_1 and e_2 can be combined to form a single expression by using the comma operator:

$$e_1, \ e_2$$

The left-hand expression e_1 is evaluated first. The type and value of a "comma expression" is the type and value of the right-hand expression e_2. Note that the commas separating the variables in definitions and declarations, and separating the arguments in function calls are not instances of the comma operator. Comma expressions must be enclosed in parentheses in situations where their use can lead to ambiguous interpretations. For example, when a comma expression is used as a function argument, then it must be enclosed within parentheses.

As an illustration of the comma operator, consider the function *palindrome* given below which determines whether or not a string is palindromic. A palindrome string reads the same whether it is read from left to right or from right to left; for example, strings "mom" and "123454321" are palindromes. Function *palindrome*, which is shown below, returns 1 if its argument *s* is palindromic; otherwise, it returns 0 (stored in file *pal.c*):

```
#include <string.h>
int palindrome(char s[])
      /*s is the same as reverse(s)*/
{
      int i, j;

      for (i=0, j=strlen(s)-1; i<j; i++, j--)
          if (s[i] != s[j]) return 0;
      return 1;
}
```

The *for* loop statement header takes three arguments: an initial-value expression, a termination condition, and a next-value expression. The comma operator is used in the above *for* statement to combine two initial-value expressions and two next-value expressions into single expressions. This example also illustrates the versatility of the C *for* statement when compared to the FORTRAN DO statement: with the help of the comma operator, the *for* statement can have two loop variables and two loop increments. This is not possible in FORTRAN.

5.1.14 SYNOPSIS OF OPERATOR PRECEDENCE & ASSOCIATIVITY. The operators are listed in groups of decreasing precedence order:

class	operators	association
postfix	() [] -> . ++ --	left to right
unary	! ~ + - ++ -- (*type*) * & sizeof	right to left
cast	(*type*)	right to left
multiplication	* / %	left to right
addition	+ -	left to right
bit shift	<< >>	left to right
relational	< <= > >=	left to right
equality	== !=	left to right
bit and	&	left to right
bit incl. or	^	left to right
bit excl. or	|	left to right
logical and	&&	left to right
logical or	||	left to right
conditional	?:	right to left
assignment	= += -= *= /= %= >>= <<= &= ^= |=	right to left
comma	,	left to right

5.2 EXPRESSIONS

An *expression* is a combination of variables, constants, function calls, operators, and parentheses.

5.2.1 CONSTANT EXPRESSIONS. Constant expressions are expressions that evaluate to a constant and, moreover, this evaluation can be done at compile time. C requires constant expressions in many places: in array bounds, in variable initializers, as labels of the *switch* statement alternatives, and in the C preprocessor #*if* statement.

Constant expressions are expressions formed by using only integer, character, and enumeration constants, the *sizeof* operator, the binary operators

+ - * / * & | ^ << >> == != < > <= >=

the unary operators

- ~

the ternary operator

?:

and the preprocessor operator *defined*.

Parentheses can be used for grouping subexpressions. The unary operator & can be used in initializers, but the *sizeof* operator cannot be used in constructing constant expressions to be used in the C preprocessor *#if* statement.

5.2.2 EXPRESSION EVALUATION. An expression is evaluated in the order specified by the operator precedence and the associativity (grouping) rules of the programming language. As in FORTRAN, C expressions may be enclosed within parentheses to override the precedence and associativity rules and to force expression evaluation in a specific order. (In K&R C, parentheses cannot be used to force evaluation of expressions in a specific order.)

6. VARIABLE INITIALIZATION

Variables can be initialized by using assignment statements in both FORTRAN and C. In addition, both languages provide special facilities just for initializing variables. In C, variables can be initialized by simply listing the initial values right after the variables in their definitions.

Fundamental type and pointer variables are initialized with an initializer of the form

= *expression*

In case of *external* and *static* (see Chapter 4) variables, the initializing expressions must be constant expressions.

Arrays (and structures, which are discussed in Chapter 3) are initialized using one of the following three forms of initializers:

= { *list-of-expressions* }

= { *list-of-expressions* , }

= "*sequence-of-characters*"

The second initializer form is used if a value is not given for each element of the array (or for each component of the structure); elements for which an initial value is not given are initialized to 0. The values in the initial list are separated by commas. Each value can be a constant expression or, if appropriate, a list of constant expressions enclosed in curly braces. The third form is used when assigning a string literal to a character array.

Here are some examples of variables initialized in their definitions:

```
char delim = ':';
int i, j = 0, nb = MAX*WORD_SIZE;
int f[] = {1, 2, 3};
float y[MAX] = {1.0, 1.0,};
int x[3][2] = {{1, 2}, {3, 4}, {5, 6}};
char fmt[] = "Number of employees = %d\n";
```

MAX and *WORD_SIZE* are symbolic constant names. If the size of an array is not specified, as in the case of the character array *fmt*, then its size will be computed by the C compiler by counting the number of initial values that have been given for the array elements. Notice that character arrays can be initialized to string literals.

Uninitialized static and external variables are guaranteed to start off with a zero initial value. Uninitialized automatic and register variables have garbage values: they must be initialized before they are used.

7. STATEMENTS

Although there are many cosmetic differences between the executable statements in FORTRAN and C, the statements in these two languages by and large provide similar functionality. FORTRAN statements must not begin in columns 1 through 6. There is no such requirement in C. Statements in both languages can be labeled. C labels are identifiers, not numbers as in FORTRAN. This allows the use of mnemonic labels. Unlike FORTRAN statements, every C statement, except executable statements ending with a right curly brace (i.e., compound statements), must be terminated by a semicolon.

7.1 EXPRESSIONS & STATEMENTS

In C, unlike in FORTRAN and in most other languages, any expression can be converted into a statement simply by appending a semicolon to it. The value of the expression is then simply discarded.

7.2 NULL STATEMENT

A semicolon by itself represents the null statement. In C, a null statement is used in places where the syntax requires the presence of a statement but where a statement is not really necessary. As an example of the use of a null statement, consider the function *strcpy* (stored in file *strcpy.c*), which mimics the functionality of the C library function with the same name:

```
char *strcpy(char d[], char s[])
{
    int i;

    for (i=0; i<strlen(s); d[i]=s[i], i++)
        ;
    return d;
}
```

The body of the *for* loop consists of a null statement; all the work is done in the expressions given in the loop header. The *null* statement is useful in C because it often allows much work to be conveniently done by expressions which in other languages is done using statements.

Notice the use of the comma operator in the *for* statement header to combine two expressions into one. Of course, the *for* statement could also have been written without the comma operator as

```
for (i=0; i<strlen(s); i++)
        d[i] = s[i];
```

which just goes to show the flexibility of C to support a variety of programming paradigms.

7.3 ASSIGNMENT STATEMENT

Because C provides the assignment operator, it does not provide a specific statement for assignment as provided in FORTRAN. An assignment statement is readily constructed in C by appending a semicolon to an assignment expression as in

```
a = 0;
max = a > b ? a : b;
```

In this case, the value of the assignment expression is discarded. However, the fact that assignment is an operator allows multiple assignments to be written as a single statement:

```
a = b = 1;
```

The assignment operator associates from the right, so the effect of the above multiple assignment is to first assign 1 to *b*, and then assign the result of the first assignment (that is, 1) to *a*. Remember that the result of an assignment expression is the value assigned to the variable.

Assignment statements can also be constructed using the compound assignment operators. For example,

```
a[i] += x*y;
i <<= 5;
```

Because assignment is an operator in C, assignments are often used in expressions to write compact code. For example, in the conditional expression of the following *if* statement, a file is opened by calling function *fopen*. This function returns a "file pointer" which is assigned to the variable *db*. If the value returned by *fopen* is the null pointer, then an error message is printed:

```
if ((db = fopen("database", "r")) == NULL)
        error("cannot open database");
```

Assignments cannot be used like this in FORTRAN. In FORTRAN, two separate statements would have to be used: an assignment followed by an *IF* statement.

7.4 UNRESTRICTED GOTO STATEMENTS

The one thing that is immediately obvious upon looking at FORTRAN programs is the pervasive nature of the *GOTO* statements. The FORTRAN *GOTO* statement is an unrestricted *GOTO* statement because it can be used to jump to any place in the program. Unrestricted *GOTO* statements are recognized as bad for programming because they make programs harder to understand and debug. Consequently, the "structured" programming languages provide facilities that make the use of *GOTO* statements essentially unnecessary.

The reasons for the pervasive use of the *GOTO* statements in FORTRAN are the lack of a multi-way branching facility (like the C *switch* statement), the lack of controlled jumps from loops (like those provided by the C *break* and *continue* statement), the lack of *while* loop, and so forth.

Unrestricted *goto* statements are rarely seen in well-written C programs. Instead, programmers use restricted versions of the *goto* statement, the *break* and *continue* statements. We will discuss these statements later. In this section, we will discuss the C *goto* statement. Targets of *goto* statements are C executable statements (not definitions and declarations, or C preprocessor statements), which must be explicitly labeled with a prefix of the form

label:

where *label* is an identifier. As mentioned earlier, the use of identifiers instead of numbers for labels allows programmers to use mnemonic labels.

The *goto* statement itself has the form

goto *label*;

7.5 IF STATEMENT

The C *if* statement is similar to the FORTRAN block *IF* statement. But C does not have the counterpart of the FORTRAN arithmetic *IF* statement. Here is the C *if* statement, with and without the *else* clause:

```
if (expression) statement
```

```
if (expression) statement else statement
```

Unless the *if* statement is small, it is not given on a single line. For example, to enhance readability, *if* statements are often written as

```
if (expression)
    statement
```

```
if (expression)
    statement
else
    statement
```

Notice that the C *if* statement requires that the *if* expression be enclosed in parentheses and that there is no keyword corresponding to the FORTRAN keyword *THEN*.

The conditional operator is often used instead of the *if* statement for many simple cases. For example, the following *if* statement

```
if (a < b)
    max = b;
else
    max = a;
```

is often written as

```
max = a < b ? b : a;
```

Like FORTRAN block *IF* statements, C *if* statements can be nested. C statements do not have the counterpart of the *END IF* statement. Consequently, when nesting *if* statements there can be ambiguity regarding which *if* statement should an *else* clause be paired with. If a nested *if* statement in C has more *if* clauses than *else* clauses, then any resulting ambiguity is resolved by matching each *else* clause with the closest and innermost *if* clause that has not been matched as yet.

As an example of nested *if* statements in C, consider the following function *grade* that takes a numeric grade (between 0 and 100) and converts it to a letter grade (stored in file *grade.c*):

```
char grade(int i)
{
    if (i > 100 || i < 0) {
        printf("grade:error, bad score=%d\n",i);
        exit(1);
    }
    else if (i > 85)
        return 'A';
    else if (i > 70)
        return 'B';
    else if (i > 55)
        return 'C';
    else if (i > 40)
        return 'D';
    else
        return 'F';
}
```

Curly braces are used in the true alternative of the *if* statement to combine two statements into one logical statement. Remember that the C syntax allows only a single statement each for the *if* alternatives. The *exit* function call terminates the program.

Notice that judicious use of indentation improves program readability. The indentation style used here for the nested *if* statements is not the same as shown earlier; there is no need to be rigid. You may use any reasonable indentation style, but whatever style you use, be consistent.

7.6 LOOP STATEMENTS

Unlike FORTRAN, C has three kinds of loop statements: the *while* statement, the *do-while* statement, and the *for* statement. The *for* statement is the counterpart of the FORTRAN *DO* statement, but the *for* statement is more powerful and versatile than the *DO* statement. C's loop statements are discussed in the next chapter.

8. FUNCTIONS

Unlike FORTRAN, C does not differentiate between functions that return values and functions that do not (like the FORTRAN subroutines). Functions that do not return a value are declared as functions with the result type *void*.

FORTRAN provides a large number of pre-defined functions which are called intrinsic functions. C also provides a large number of pre-defined functions but they are called standard library functions.

C provides two sets of facilities for writing functions: pure functions and macros. We have seen many examples of functions by now; they will be discussed in detail in Chapter 4. The macro facility is provided by the C preprocessor. Macros are like functions except that macro calls are replaced textually, before the compilation phase, by their bodies after appropriately substituting arguments for the corresponding parameters. Macros are essentially in-line functions. Macros are faster than functions, because they avoid the need for instructions for jumping to and returning from the functions. However, there is a price that may have to be paid for this speedup: the macro bodies replacing the calls can take up more storage. Macros will be discussed in detail in Chapter 6.

9. INPUT/OUTPUT

Both FORTRAN and C provide a wide variety of facilities for reading from and writing to files, reading from the keyboard and writing to the display. FORTRAN input/output (I/O) facilities are built-in the language and FORTRAN provides statements for interacting directly with the computer hardware such as the keyboard and the display. C does not provide I/O statements. All I/O, including that for interacting with the computer hardware, is done by calling standard library routines.

There are three files that are automatically made available to every C program. These are the standard input, the standard output, and the standard error files. The standard input file is associated, by default, with the keyboard, and can be explicitly referenced by the name *stdin*. This identifier is defined in the standard input header file *stdio.h*. Similarly, standard output and error files are both associated with the display. They can be explicitly referenced using the names *stdout* and *stderr* which are also defined in *stdio.h*. (Note that *stdin*, *stdout*, and *stderr* are constants of type *FILE* *.) Normal output is written to *stdout*. Error messages are written to *stderr* so they can be separated from the normal output by redirecting *stdout* or *stderr*.

Many C programs are written so that they read input from *stdin* and write output to *stdout*. Standard I/O redirection is used to read from a file instead of the keyboard and write to a file instead of the display.

As an example of I/O and I/O redirection, consider the following program (stored in file *roots.c*) for computing the roots of a quadratic equation:

```c
#include <stdio.h>
#include <math.h>

char f1[]="error, coeff %g, %g, %g have complex roots\n";
char f2[]="coeff = %g, %g, %g, roots = %g, %g\n";
main(void)
{
    double a, b, c, r1, r2, tmp;
    int n;

    while ((n=scanf("%lf%lf%lf", &a, &b, &c))==3){
        if ((tmp = b*b - 4*a*c) < 0) {
            fprintf(stderr, f1, a, b, c);
            continue;
        }
        else
            tmp = sqrt(tmp);
        r1 = (-b+tmp)/(2*a);
        r2 = (-b-tmp)/(2*a);
        printf(f2, a, b, c, r1, r2);
    }
    if (n != EOF) {
        fprintf(stderr,"error, missing coeff\n");
        exit(1);
    }
    exit(0);
}
```

Function *fprintf* is used for printing error messages on the standard error file, that is, on the display. Error messages are not printed on the standard output file (say by using the *printf* function) because this means that error messages will be redirected when standard output is redirected. This may delay discovery of execution errors. Also, characters written to *stderr* are usually not buffered as are characters written to *stdout*; they are printed immediately. (Buffering is used to speed up program execution by reducing the number of disk accesses.)

Note that the function call

```c
printf(fmt2, a, b, c, r1, r2)
```

is equivalent to the function call

```c
fprintf(stdout, fmt2, a, b, c, r1, r2)
```

Some other items of interest are the use of the arrays *fmt1* and *fmt2* to store the formats that will be used by the *fprintf* and *printf* function calls to print error messages, and the coefficients and the roots of the quadratic equation. Note that preprocessor constant definitions could also have been used to specify the format strings. Function *exit* is called to terminate the program explicitly. If *exit* is not called explicitly, then it will be called automatically, but its exit status (the argument supplied to *exit*) will be garbage. The exit value can be used at the

MS-DOS or UNIX command level to determine whether or not a program executed successfully.

Here is some sample input (stored in file *roots.dat*) that will be used for program *roots*:

```
1 -4 4
1 0 1
2 5 -2
2 1 7
6 3
```

Executing *roots* with this data by using the command

```
roots <roots.dat
```

produces the following output on the terminal:

```
coeff = 1, -4, 4, roots = 2, 2
error, coeff 1, 0, 1 have complex roots
coeff = 2, 5, -2, roots = 0.350781, -2.85078
error, coeff 2, 1, 7 have complex roots
error, missing coeff
```

In this case, the error messages are printed on the display even if the standard output is redirected as shown below:

```
roots <roots.dat >roots.res
```

The output produced on the display is

```
error, coeff 1, 0, 1 have complex roots
error, coeff 2, 1, 7 have complex roots
error, missing coeff
```

and the output written to file *roots.res* is

```
coeff = 1, -4, 4, roots = 2, 2
coeff = 2, 5, -2, roots = 0.350781, -2.850781
```

On the MS-DOS system, standard error output cannot be redirected; output written to the standard error file will always be displayed on the screen. On some systems, e.g., the UNIX system, standard error output can be redirected to a file just like standard output can be redirected to a file.

If you want to read from and write to files other than the standard input (*stdin*), standard output (*stdout*), and standard error (*stderr*) files, then you must follow the following steps:

1. Include the header file *stdio.h* (using the *#include* instruction).

2. Declare a *FILE* * type variable for each file.

3. Open the file for reading or writing, as appropriate, using the file open function *fopen*: this function takes as arguments the file name and a string indicating how the file is to be accessed. It returns a value that identifies the opened file. Save this value in the file variable and use this variable to access the file.

4. The file can be accessed as a stream of characters (with functions such as *fgetc*, *fscanf*, *fputc*, and *fprintf*) or as a random access file for reading and writing blocks of data at appropriate places within the file (using functions such as *fseek*, *rewind*, *fread*, and *fwrite*).

5. Finally, after file accesses have been completed, the file should be closed (using function *fclose*). If the file is not closed explicitly, then it will be closed automatically upon program termination. But remember that only a small number of files (about 15) can be open at any given time. If a large number of files are being manipulated in the program, then it is a good idea to close the files that are no longer needed.

10. COMMONLY USED INPUT/OUTPUT FUNCTIONS

A partial list of the C file access functions is given below. For a complete list and a detailed explanation of each function, see the Appendix. These file access functions can be classified into three categories: input, output, and file manipulation and file status query.

First, here are the input functions:

fgets	Get a string from a file.
fread	Read blocks from a file.
getc	Get a character from a file.
getchar	Get a character from *stdin*.
gets	Get a string from *stdin*.
fscanf	Read formatted input from a file.
scanf	Read formatted input from *stdin*.
sprintf	Write formatted output to a string.

Now, here are the output functions:

fprintf	Write formatted output to a file.
fputc	Write a character to a file.
fputs	Write a string to a file.
fwrite	Write blocks to a file.

printf   Write formatted output to *stdout*.

putc   Write a character to a file.

putchar   Write a character to *stdout*.

puts   Write a string to *stdout*.

sscanf   Read formatted input from a string.

Finally, here are the file manipulation and file status query functions:

fclose   Close a file.

feof   End-of-file check.

ferror   Error check.

fflush   Flush output buffer.

fopen   Open a file.

11. ERROR TRAPPING

FORTRAN does not provide mechanism for handling errors (such as a divide/by zero) other than I/O errors. FORTRAN error handling must be specified in the I/O statement. This action is simply a jump to a statement (where the appropriate error handling action is taken). By contrast, in C I/O errors are detected by examining the value returned by the I/O function. Values indicating an error are specified as part of the function's behavior. In fact, this paradigm is routinely used by most C functions to indicate an error.

Unlike FORTRAN, C provides a mechanism that can be used to catch and handle errors and exception conditions (such as division by zero and floating-point overflow) which raise a signal (interrupt). A signal handler function is associated with a signal by calling the function *signal*. This function is then called automatically when the signal associated with it is raised. Signal handling is discussed in Chapter 4.

12. PROGRAM TERMINATION

C programs can terminate in three different ways: by completing execution of the *main* function, by calling the *exit* function, or by executing the *return* statement in the *main* function.

Function *exit*, like the *END* statement, closes all open files. It also cleans the output buffers causing buffered items to be written to appropriate files. *exit* is called with a zero argument to indicate successful (normal) termination and with a non-zero argument to indicate error or abnormal termination.

13. EXERCISES

1. The following C loop exploits the fact that the && operator evaluates its
    second argument only when *i* is less than *n* to avoid a subscript error:

    ```
    for (i=0; i<n && a[i] != x; i++)
        ;
    ```

    How will you write this C loop in FORTRAN?

2. Write a C function *max* that computes the maximum element of a
    floating-point array. Test it by writing a *main* function that defines and
    initializes an array, then calls *max* with the array as an argument, and then
    prints the maximum value in the array.

3. Write a small C program to print the number of bytes used by your C
    compiler to implement the *char, int, long int, short int, float,* and *double*
    types. (Hint: use the *sizeof* operator.)

CHAPTER 3

C FACILITIES NOT IN FORTRAN

The goal of this chapter is to discuss C facilities for which there are no direct counterparts in FORTRAN. Some of the important facilities such as the facilities provided by the C preprocessor, pointers, and functions will be briefly described in this chapter, but they will be discussed in detail in later chapters.

1. C PREPROCESSOR

The C preprocessor is a simple macro preprocessor that processes the C source text before it is parsed and compiled [Harb84]. In some C environments, the C preprocessor and the C compiler are physically implemented as separate programs while in others the C preprocessor is integrated with the C compiler. C preprocessor facilities are an important part of the C programmer's repertoire. So far, we have seen two major facilities of the C preprocessor: file inclusion (the *#include* instruction) and constant definition (the *#define* instruction). In addition to these facilities, the preprocessor has facilities for conditional compilation and macros (in-line functions). FORTRAN does not have counterparts of many of the facilities provided by the C preprocessor. We shall defer detailed discussion of the C preprocessor facilities to Chapter 6.

2. TYPES

2.1 TYPE DEFINITIONS

The C type definition mechanism, the *typedef* statement, allows the user to give symbolic names to types constructed using pre-defined or other user-defined types. The *typedef* statement has the form

typedef *type* *type-name*

where *type* can be a type name or the description of a type.

Here are some examples of type definitions:

```
typedef unsigned word;
typedef double length;
typedef struct {int a, b;} pair;
        /*structures will be discussed later*/
```

Type names declared using the *typedef* mechanism can be used to define (declare) variables just as they can be defined (declared) with the pre-defined types such as *int* and *double*. Here are some examples illustrating the use of the above types to define variables:

```
word x, w[M];   /*M is a user-defined constant*/
length l1, l2;
pair *p;   /*the asterisk specifies a pointer*/
```

2.2 FUNDAMENTAL TYPES

There are several C fundamental types that are not in FORTRAN: the *void* type, the *unsigned* types, and the *enumeration* type.

2.2.1 VOID TYPE. The *void* (empty) type, which we have seen used before, is a recent addition to C [Harb84]. The *void* type does not have any values or any operations associated with it. It is used primarily for specifying parameterless functions and functions that do not return results (i.e., subroutines). For example, the function declaration

```
int date(void);
```

specifies that *date* is a parameterless function and the function definition

```
void error(char *msg)
{
    printf("Error: %s\en", msg);
    exit(1);
}
```

specifies that *error* is a function that does not return a result.

The addition of the *void* type to the C language did not really add to its capabilities. However, its use does allow C compilers to do better type checking and it also improves program readability.

2.2.2 UNSIGNED TYPES. Unsigned types are typically used for bit manipulation and for storing positive integers whose representation requires one bit more than that possible with signed integers. Unsigned integer variables are defined (declared) by using the keyword *unsigned* in conjunction with the integer type, e.g.,

```
unsigned long max;
```

Unsigned integer arithmetic is performed modulo $n+1$, n being the largest integer that can be stored in the unsigned integer type.

2.2.3 ENUMERATION TYPES. Enumeration types allow the user to define types whose values are user-defined symbols. Here is an example of an enumeration type declaration and a variable definition that uses it:

```
enum day {sun, mon, tue, wed, thu, fri, sat};
enum day d;
```

The identifier *day* is called the enumeration tag. Identifiers *sun, mon*, etc., are called enumeration constants which are of type *int*. The value of an enumeration constant is its position in the definition of an enumeration tag (or an enumeration type). For example, the value of *sun* is 0 and that of *mon* is 1.

Because of the presence of the keyword *enum*, enumeration type variable definitions that use enumeration tags do not look quite the same as definitions involving fundamental types such as *int*. However, enumeration types declared using the *typedef* facility do not have this problem. For instance, type *day* and variable *d* could alternatively have been declared and defined respectively as

```
typedef enum {
    sun, mon, tue, wed, thu, fri, sat
} day;
day d;
```

Variable *d* can be assigned values of type *day* as in the assignment

```
d = sun;
```

Here is an example illustrating the use of the above enumeration variable:

```
if (d == sun || d == sat)
    total_pay += daily_wage * 1.5;
else
    total_pay += daily_wage;
```

The above statement could have been written alternatively as

```
total_pay+=daily_wage*((d==sun||d==sat)?1.5:1);
```

Enumeration types, like the *void* type, are a recent addition to C. The *typedef* mechanism is also a recent addition to C and it makes the enumeration tag mechanism redundant.

2.3 DERIVED TYPES

Derived types are types built using the fundamental types: There are four derived types in C: arrays, structures, unions, and pointers. C arrays are similar to FORTRAN arrays but there are some differences. And there are no counterparts of structures, unions, and pointers in FORTRAN.

2.3.1 ARRAYS. Multi-dimensional arrays in C are simply arrays whose elements are arrays. An element of a *n*-dimensional array is referenced, as in FORTRAN, by supplying *n* subscripts. However, in C these subscripts are given individually, i.e., enclosed separately in square brackets, while in FORTRAN all the subscripts specifying an element are enclosed in one pair of parentheses. A sub-array of a *n*-dimensional array is referenced by specifying less than *n* subscripts. As an example, consider the three-dimensional array *a* declared as:

```
int a[5][5][5];
```

a refers to the whole array and $a[i][j][k]$ refers to a single element of *a*. $a[i]$ refers to the two-dimensional sub-array of *a* whose elements are the elements of *a* with the first subscript equal to *i*. Similarly, $a[i][j]$ refers to a one-dimensional sub-array of *a* whose elements are the elements of *a* with the first subscript equal to *i* and the second subscript equal to *j*.

2.3.2 STRUCTURES. Structures, like arrays, are used to give a group of related variables a collective name. Unlike arrays, components of structures can have different types. Suppose you want to collect employee information such as name, id, age, sex, and the name of the employee's manager. In FORTRAN, one array will be declared for each of the above items and the ith element of each array will contain appropriate information about the ith employee. In C, one array with elements of a user-defined type *employee* can be defined and all information about one employee can be stored in one element of this array. The encapsulation provided by C structures makes it very easy to handle and manipulate groups of related data items.

A structure type has the form

```
struct tag {
     structure component declarations
}
```

The structure tag, which gives a symbolic name to a structure, is optional. Structure tags are similar to enumeration tags. Structures can be used like other types to define and declare identifiers.

Here are some examples:

```
struct {
    char *name;   /*pointer to name*/
    int id, age, sex;
    char *mngr_name;
} a, emp[MAX], *p;

struct {double x, y;} p1, p2;
```

```
struct employee {
    char *name;
    int id, age, sex;
    char *mngr_name;
};
struct coordinate {double x, y;};

struct employee a, emp[MAX], *p;
struct coordinate p1, p2;
```

The keyword *struct* must be used when using structure tags to define or declare variables. However, this keyword is not used when using structure type names defined with the C type definition facility *typedef*. This facility duplicates the structure tag mechanism making it almost, but not quite, redundant. As shown later, structure tags are still necessary for defining recursive structures.

Here are some examples of structure type names specified with the *typedef* facility and examples illustrating their use:

```
typedef struct {
    char make[N], model[N];
    int year;
    float cc, hp;
} automobile;

typedef struct {
    double r, i;
} complex;

automobile a, b;
complex c, d;
```

Structure type names, rather than structure tags, are more like the pre-defined type names such as *int* and *double*.

Structure components are referenced using the selected component notation which has the form

structure-name . component-name

Here are some examples of structure components (using the variable definitions given above):

```
c.x
c.y
a.make
(*p).name
```

C provides a convenient notation for referencing structure components that involve a pointer to the structure. Using this notation, the last example shown above can be written alternatively as

```
p->name
```

C supports structure assignment, allows structures to be given as arguments in function calls, and structures can be returned as function results. Global (that is, external or file static) structure variables can be given initial values when they are defined.

As mentioned above, the *typedef* mechanism has not completely eliminated the need for structure tags. They are still necessary for defining a recursive structure such as

```
struct student {
    char first, last[MAX];
    int id;
    float gpa;
    struct student *next;
};
```

Even if the *typedef* declaration had been used, a structure tag would still be necessary:

```
typedef struct student {
    char first, last[MAX];
    int id;
    float gpa;
    struct student *next;
} student;
```

The same name, *student* in the above example, can be used for both the structure tag and the type name because structure tags and type names occupy different "name spaces". Variables of type *student* can be declared using the type *student* or the tag *student*.

As an example illustrating the use of structures, we will write a pair of functions to add and multiply values of type *complex* (stored in file *complex.c*):

```
#include "complex.h"

complex add(complex a, complex b)
{
    complex c;
    c.r = a.r+b.r;
    c.i = a.i+b.i;
    return c;
}

complex mul(complex a, complex b)
{
    complex c;
    c.r = a.r*b.r - a.i*b.i;
    c.i = a.r+b.i + a.i*b.r;
    return c;
}
```

File *complex.h* contains the declaration of the type *complex* which is declared as shown earlier, that is, as

```
typedef struct {
    double r, i;
} complex;
```

Here are some examples illustrating the use of the *complex* functions shown above:

```
complex x, y, z;
    ...
z = add(x, mul(y, z));
```

2.3.3 UNIONS. Unions are used for allocating multiple objects, called the union components, on the same storage area. That is, unions are used to overlay storage. This allows a storage area to be interpreted, in multiple ways, according to the type of the union components.

Unions are similar to structures with regard to definitions, declarations, and component selection. The main difference is that all the union components, unlike structure components, are mapped to the same storage. Here is what a union type looks like:

```
union tag {
    component₁;
    component₂;
    ...
    componentₙ;
}
```

$$\text{union } tag \; \{$$
$$\quad component_1;$$
$$\quad component_2;$$
$$\quad ...$$
$$\quad component_n;$$
$$\}$$

The union tag, like the structure tag, is optional. Like structure types, union types can be defined using the *typedef* statement.

As an example of storage overlay using unions, consider a union named *point*, given below, which allows the position of a point to be specified either in terms of cartesian or polar coordinates:

```
union {
    struct {double x, y;} cartesian;
    struct {double r, theta;} polar;
} point;
```

Components of this union are accessed as

```
point.cartesian.x
point.cartesian.y
point.polar.r
point.polar.theta
```

The value stored in *point* will either be in cartesian coordinates or in polar coordinates. In the first case the *cartesian* component structure will be used to access or update this value while in the second case the *polar* component structure will be used. Another variable, say *kind*, must be used to note the type of coordinates currently being used to store the position in union *point*. And uses of the value of variable *point* must be based on the value of the "indicator" variable *kind*. For example,

```
switch (kind) {
case 0: use the cartesian structure of union point;
case 1: use the polar structure of union point;
}
```

2.3.4 POINTERS. A *pointer* value refers to a specific location in memory. This value can be the address of a variable, of a function, or of just a block of storage. C allows the programmer to manipulate pointer values: pointer variables can be declared and pointer arithmetic is allowed. Pointers are used in C to

- pass addresses of variables as arguments to functions to allow them to change variable values (to simulate passing arguments by reference as in FORTRAN). Also, in case of large objects, passing a pointer to an object is more efficient than passing the whole object because it requires less storage for the parameter and because it avoids copying of the large object to the parameter.

- implement dynamic structures such as lists, which are much more flexible and efficient than arrays for keeping lists of items from which items are frequently deleted and to which items are frequently added.

- read from and write to specific locations in memory, subject to any constraints imposed by the operating system.

Pointers are defined (declared) by using the dereferencing operator *. Here are some examples:

```
char *p;
FILE *fp;
struct {double x, y;} *pc;
int *a[10], (*b)[10];
double **pd;
char *line(void);
```

Variables *p*, *fp*, and *pc* are respectively defined as pointers of type *char*, *FILE*, and the structure given in the definition. Variable *a* is defined as an array of integer pointers and variable *b* is defined as a pointer to an array of integers. Notice that parentheses are used in the definition of *b* to ensure that *b* is bound to the dereferencing operator * and not to the subscript operator []. Variable *pd* is defined as a pointer of type pointer to a *double* object. Finally, *line* is declared as a function that does not take any arguments and returns a character pointer as its result.

Objects pointed to by pointers are referenced by using the dereferencing operator * which, as we saw above, is also used for defining (declaring) pointer variables. Here are some examples which use the definitions and the function declaration given above:

p	Pointer to an integer object.
*p	The integer object pointed to by *p*.
(*pc).*x*	The *x* component of the structure pointed to by *pc*.
*a[*i*]	The integer object pointed to by the ith element of *a*.
(*b)[*i*]	The ith element of the array pointed to by *b*.
*pd	Pointer to a *double* object.
malloc(*n*)	The void pointer result returned by the function *malloc*.

Pointers are frequently used to point to structures. C provides the indirect selection operator -> for simplifying the notation used to access structure components. For example, as mentioned earlier, instead of accessing component *x* of the structure pointed to by the pointer variable *pc* as

```
(*pc).x
```

it can be accessed using the operator -> as

```
pc->x
```

C definitions and declarations can sometimes be hard to understand. The one important thing to remember is that the notation used for defining and declaring a variable mirrors the notation used for referencing the variable. For a detailed discussion of C definitions and declarations, and how to understand complex definitions and declarations, see *C: An Advanced Introduction* [Geha88].

It is important to note that the storage for objects referenced by pointers is not allocated automatically. A pointer definition allocates storage for the pointer but not for the object pointed to by the pointer. Storage for the object referred to by a pointer must be allocated explicitly. We shall discuss storage allocation in Chapter 5 which discusses pointers in detail. A pointer variable can also be made to point to the address of a previously defined variable. Here are some examples of assignments to pointer variables:

```
#include <stdio.h>
#include <stddef.h>
char *s;
int *pi, i, n;
employee *p, *q;
   ...
if ((s = malloc(n)) == NULL) { ... }
pi = &i;
p = q;
```

The constant identifier *NULL* denotes the null pointer; it is defined in the header file *stddef.h* typically as

```
#define NULL 0
```

The null pointer *NULL* can be assigned to a pointer variable of any type. By convention, functions that return a pointer value, such as *malloc*, return the null pointer *NULL* to indicate an error or a terminating condition.

In the assignment "*pi* = &*i*", the pointer variable *pi* is assigned the address of variable *i*. (The *address of* operator "&" extracts the address of its operand.) After this assignment **pi* and *i* become synonyms for each other because both of them refer to the same integer object. The value of variable *i* can now also be changed by using the pointer *pi*. For example, the assignment

```
*pi = 5;
```

changes the value of variable *i* to 5.

Similarly, after the assignment "*p* = *q*", **p* and **q* become synonyms for each other because they both refer to the same object (of type *employee*).

Now let us look at one common example of the use of pointers in C: to simulate passing arguments by reference as is done in FORTRAN. We will write a function to exchange the values of two integers. Here is a first attempt to write such a swap function:

```
void swapi(int a, int b)   /*incorrect*/
{
    int tmp;

    tmp = a;
    a = b;
    b = tmp;
}
```

Suppose we call *swapi* with two integer variables *x* and *y*:

```
swapi(x, y);
```

This version of *swapi* does not work. When called with two variables, say *x* and *y*, to be swapped, *swapi* copies their values into parameters *a* and *b*, and then exchanges the values of *a* and *b*. Meanwhile, the values of variables *x* and *y* remain unchanged because all arguments are passed by value in C. To ensure that the values of the two integer variables are exchanged, *swapi* must be modified so that it is called with the addresses of *x* and *y*:

```
swapi(&x, &y);
```

The addresses of *x* and *y* will now be stored in the parameters *a* and *b*. Using the addresses of *x* and *y*, their values can now be changed. Here is the modified version of *swapi*:

```
void swapi(int *a, int *b)
{
    int tmp;

    tmp = *a;
    *a = *b;
    *b = tmp;
}
```

The modified version uses the addresses in *a* and *b* to change the values of the arguments to be swapped (*x* and *y* in this example). Note that *a* contains the address of *x*; therefore, **a* is a synonym for *x*. Similarly, **b* is a synonym for *y*.

Functions for swapping other fundamental type variables can be written by trivially modifying this function. By using an extra parameter, a general swap function that swaps arguments of any type, including arrays of any size, can be easily written in C. We shall defer discussion of the general swap function to Chapter 4.

Pointers are an important aspect of C. We have discussed them briefly here to give you an idea about what pointers are and what they are used for. There is a close and mutually beneficial relationship between pointers and arrays (and therefore strings). Pointers are discussed in more detail in Chapter 5.

2.4 TYPE QUALIFIERS

C has two type qualifiers: *const* and *volatile*. The types of variables that are to be read only and not to be updated are qualified with the keyword *const*. Such variables cannot be assigned values. Consequently, *const* variables must be initialized in their definitions. Here are some examples:

```
const double pi = 3.1416;
const char fname[] = "database";
```

Some variables are associated with hardware locations. Reading values of these variables and writing values to these variables causes hardware actions such as transmission of values to a display or the generation of an interrupt. This information is given to compilers so that they do not try to optimize references to such variables. For example, suppose that characters are displayed on a terminal by writing to memory location 500 as shown below:

```
volatile char *out;
char c;
    ...
out = (char *) 500; /*out now refers to location 500*/
    ...
*out = c; ...   *out = c;
```

Suppose that these were the only references to *out* in the program, and *out* was not declared to be of a *volatile* type. Under these circumstances, an optimizing compiler may through out all references to *out* because as far as it is concerned *out* does not serve any purpose. Unless such variables are specified to be volatile, the compiler has no way of knowing that assigning values to these variables causes hardware actions such as displaying the values assigned to *out* on the screen.

3. OPERATORS

As mentioned earlier, C has many more operators than FORTRAN some of which do not have cannot be written easily in FORTRAN. Operators were discussed in detail in Chapter 1 and C operators for which there are no counterparts in FORTRAN were also discussed in detail there. However, because this chapter is about C facilities that are not in FORTRAN, I will briefly discuss the C operators for which FORTRAN does not have counterparts.

FORTRAN does not have operators for selecting structure components because it does not support structures. It also does not have operators for incrementing or decrementing variables, or the compound assignment operators but these operators can be trivially implemented using assignment.

Because FORTRAN does not support pointers, it does not provide operators for manipulating pointers. It also does not have a *sizeof* operator which is typically used for dynamic storage allocation in conjunction with pointers.

FORTRAN does not have a cast operator but it does provide functions for converting between the arithmetic types. There is no remainder operator but the remainder can be easily computed by using integer division. FORTRAN does not have any bit manipulation operators because it was designed to move the programmer away from thinking in terms of bits.

FORTRAN's logical operators are unconditional in that the second operand is evaluated regardless of the value of the first operand. C's logical operators are conditional in that the second operator is evaluated only when necessary.

FORTRAN does not have the conditional operator which is sort of an abbreviated version of an *if* statement that can be used within an expression. Finally, FORTRAN does not have the comma operator which is used to combine two expressions into one. C is partially an expression-oriented language where such an operator can be put to good use as illustrated in the previous chapter. FORTRAN is a purely statement-oriented language and there is no place in such a language for a comma operator.

4. STATEMENTS

I will now discuss the C statements for which there are no FORTRAN counterparts.

4.1 GROUPING STATEMENTS INTO ONE LOGICAL STATEMENT

Curly braces can be used in C to combine several statements into one logical (compound) statement. This is necessary when several statements must be given in places, such as in the *if* and *while* statements, where the C syntax allows only a single statement. The compound statement is very flexible: it can be as long as necessary, it can contain nested compound statements, and it can span as many lines as necessary.

Finally, one can even define new variables at the beginning of the compound statement. The scope of these variables is restricted to the body of the compound statement. As an example of the use of a compound statement to define local variables, consider the following code that exchanges the values of two integer variables:

```
    ...
{
    int tmp;

    tmp = n;
    n = i;
    i = tmp;
}
    ...
```

The scope of variable *tmp* is restricted to the compound statement. *tmp* cannot be accessed outside the compound statement.

4.2 RESTRICTED GOTO STATEMENTS: BREAK & CONTINUE

FORTRAN does not have any restricted (controlled) *goto* statements while C has two: *break* and *continue*. The *break* statement is used in loops and in the *switch* multi-way branch statement. The effect of executing the *break* statement is to exit the immediately surrounding loop or the *switch* statement.

Like the FORTRAN *CONTINUE* statement, the C *continue* statement is used only in loops. But its semantics are very different. The *continue* statement causes the current loop iteration to be abandoned by jumping to the end of the loop body and then begin the next iteration (if allowed by the loop condition).

4.3 SWITCH STATEMENT

The C *switch* statement is a multi-way branch statement; there is no counterpart of this statement in FORTRAN although the computed *GOTO* statement can be used to easily implement equivalent functionality.

The *switch* statement has the form

```
switch (exp) {
case-label₁:   statements₁
case-label₂:   statements₂
   ...
case-labelₙ:   statementsₙ
}
```

where *exp* is an integer expression and each *case-label$_i$* has either the form

```
case const
```

where *const* is an integral constant or consists of just the keyword

```
default
```

Duplicate labels are not allowed in the *switch* statement. Execution of a *switch* statement proceeds as follows: The *switch* expression *exp* is evaluated and program execution jumps to a *case* label that has an integer constant equal to *exp*; statements following the *case* label are then executed. If there is no such label, then program execution jumps to the *default* label and statements following the label are then executed. If there is no matching *case* label and there is no *default* label, then the *switch* statement behaves like the null statement.

As an example, consider the following *switch* statement [Harb84]:

```
switch (x) {
   case 1: printf("*\n");
   case 2: printf("**\n");
   case 3: printf("***\n");
   case 4: printf("****\n");
}
```

If x has the value 1, then 10 asterisks will be printed, if it has the value 2 then 9 asterisks will be printed, and so on. This is because execution of an alternative (one of the *printf* statements in this example) does not complete execution of the *switch* statement; instead, the remaining alternatives are then executed. To leave the *switch* statement right after executing an alternative, a *break* statement must be given explicitly as the last statement in the alternative:

```
switch (x) {
   case 1: printf("*\n");
           break;
   case 2: printf("**\n");
           break;
   case 3: printf("***\n");
           break;
   case 4: printf("****\n");
           break;
}
```

Now, if x has the value i (between 1 and 4), then only i asterisks will be printed.

To execute only the statements associated with a *case* label, the following form of the *switch* statement should be used:

```
switch (exp) {
   case const: statements
               break;
   case const: statements
               break;
   ...
   case const: statements
               break;
   default:    statements
}
```

There is no need to give a *break* statement after the *default* alternative because, as shown above, it is given as the last alternative. Instead of using the *break* statement to exit from a *switch* statement alternative, you can, if appropriate, also exit by using the *continue* or *return* statements. The effect of exiting with the *continue* statement is to go on to the next iteration (if allowed by the loop conditions) of the immediately enclosing loop and the effect of exiting with the *return* statement is to return from the function containing the *switch* statement.

A *switch* statement can have multiple *case* labels for the same alternative, but there must be no duplicate *case* labels.

As mentioned previously, the FORTRAN computed *GOTO* statement can be used to implement the equivalent of the C *switch* statement. But this simulation will not be as elegant as using the *switch* statement especially because of the reliance on *GOTO*s and jumps to non-mnemonic statement numbers.

As another example of the *switch* statement, consider the following program (stored in file *wc.c*) which counts the total number of characters, words, lines, spaces, tabs, and punctuation characters in the input:

```
#include <stdio.h>
#include <string.h>
main(void)
{
    int c, n = 0, nsp = 0, nwd = 0,
        nl = 0, nt = 0, np = 0;
    while ((c = getchar()) != EOF) {
        n++;
        switch (c) {
        case ' ':
            nsp++; nwd++; break;
        case '\n':
            nl++; nwd++; break;
        case '\t':
            nt++; nwd++; break;
        default:
            if (ispunct(c)) np++;
        }
    }
    printf("chars=%d, words=%d, lines=%d\n",n,nwd,nl);
    printf("spaces=%d, tabs=%d, punct=%d\n",nsp,nt,np);
}
```

The above program is straightforward and it uses a simple algorithm that does not cover all possible situations. For example, every time a space is encountered, the word count is increased by one. This strategy for counting words is fine if all the words are separated by a single space, but if there are multiple spaces between words, then the word count will be incorrect. (How will you refine the above algorithm to take care of multiple spaces between words?)

Notice that the function *ispunct* is used in the *switch* statement to avoid listing the *case* labels explicitly for each one of the punctuation characters. The reason for this is simple: listing the case labels explicitly for each of the punctuation marks will be long and tedious.

4.4 LOOP STATEMENTS: WHILE, FOR, & DO

FORTRAN has only one type of loop while C has three types of loops. Both FORTRAN and C have the *for* loops (called the *DO* loop in FORTRAN). The other two loop constructs in C are the *while* and *do-while* loops. The *while* loop executes its body as long as its test expression is true. The *do-while* loop, is like the *while* loop except that the loop test is done at the end of the loop instead of at the beginning.

4.4.1 THE WHILE LOOP. Let us start by first discussing the *while* loop. The C *while* loop has the form

```
while  (expression)  statement
```

The single statement allowed for the loop body is no restriction because curly braces can be used to combine several statements into one logical statement which can then be given as the loop body. C *while* loops can be nested.

As an example of a *while* loop, consider the following C code that sets variable i to the index of the array element whose value is equal to that of *key*; otherwise, if there is no such element, the value of i is set to *MAX* which is the size of the array:

```
while (i < MAX && a[i] != key)
    i++;
```

4.4.2 THE FOR LOOP. C has a *for* loop that is similar to the FORTRAN *DO* loop. The C *for* loop has the form

```
for  (initial-value ;  termination ;  next-value)
     statement
```

The three expressions *initial-value*, *termination*, and *next-value* control execution of the *for* loop as explained below:

1. Expression *initial-value* is evaluated at the beginning of the loop. Typically this expression is used to assign initial values to the loop variables.

2. Expression *termination* is evaluated. If this expression is true (non-zero), then the loop body is executed; otherwise, the *for* loop terminates.

3. After the loop body has been executed, expression *next-value* is evaluated. Typically this expression is used to update values of the loop variables. Execution of the loop continues with step 2.

As in the case of the *while* loop, a compound statement can be used to specify loop bodies with more than one statement.

As an example of the C *for* loop, consider the following function *sum* that computes the sum of a 2-dimensional array:

```
#define N 100
int sum(int a[][N], int m, int n)
{
    int i, j, total = 0;
    for (i=0; i<m; i++)
        for (j=0; j<n; j++)
            total += a[i][j];
    return total;
}
```

The two nested *for* loops generate a pair of indices, one for each element of the array *a*. The body of each *for* loop consists of one statement. The body of the first *for* loop is the second *for* loop. Notice that 2-dimensional arrays can be passed as arguments to functions and that only the size of the first dimension of the array can be left unspecified.

Any or all of the three *for* loop expressions can be omitted. A true value is assumed for any omitted expression. One or more of these expressions are often omitted. For example, it is common to see a loop of the form

```
for (;;) {
    ...
}
```

This loop, a "forever" or a non-terminating loop, will not terminate by itself; it must be terminated explicitly by exiting from the loop (for example, by using a *break* statement or a *return* statement).

Often a C preprocessor *#define* statement is used to make the forever nature of the loop shown above more explicit:

```
#define forever for(;;)
    ...
forever { /*forever is replaced by for(;;)*/
    ...
}
```

A non-terminating loop can also be written using the *while* statement whose expression always evaluates to true:

```
while (1) {
    ...
}
```

In FORTRAN, a non-terminating loop must be written by using *GOTO*s and *IF* statements.

The C *for* loop is much more flexible and versatile than the FORTRAN *DO* loop because the *for* loop expressions can be arbitrary expressions which can be omitted or which can consist of multiple expressions that are combined using the comma operator. To illustrate the power of the *for* loop, we will write a C program fragment to compute the square root of a floating-point number *a* using the following algorithm (due to Newton):

1. Let *new* represent the current approximation of *a*'s square root; as a first approximation of the *a*'s square root, set *new* to 0.5*a*.

2. Improve the square root approximation by setting *old* to *new* and setting *new* to 0.5*(*old*+*a*/*old*).

3. Repeat step 2 as long as necessary. Typically, a stopping point used for this iteration is when the difference between *old* and *new* becomes very small, say 0.001.

Here is a program fragment, based on the above algorithm, that computes the square root:

```
for (new=a/2, old=0.0; abs(old-new)>0.001;) {
    old = new;
    new = 0.5*(old+a/old);
}
```

Notice the absence of the *next-value* expression (the third expression) in the *for* statement. The loop variables are assigned their next values in the loop body. Alternatively, these assignments could have been made into a *next-value* expression and the loop could have been given a null body:

```
for (new=a/2, old=0.0; abs(old-new)>0.001;
                old=new, new=0.5*(old+a/old))
    ;
```

The comma operator guarantees that its left operand will be evaluated first.

4.4.3 THE DO-WHILE LOOP. The third C loop, the *do-while* loop, has the form

```
do statement while (expression);
```

The *do-while* loop executes its *body* until the specified expression becomes false. This expression is evaluated after each execution of the loop body. Consequently, the loop body is always executed at least once. This is the main difference between the *do-while* loop, and the *for* and *while* loops. As in case of the other two C loops, a compound statement can be used when the loop body consists of more than one statement.

Here is an example of the *do-while* loop in which function *send* is called at least once:

```
do send(c = getchar()); while (c != EOF);
```

5. FUNCTIONS

Unlike FORTRAN functions, C functions can be recursive. This allows programmers to write a large variety of a programs with ease. An important class of problems where recursion is particularly suitable consists of problems that can be solved by the "divide-and-conquer" approach. In this approach, a large problem is solved by splitting it into one or more smaller problems. Both large and small problems are solved by calling the same function.

Both in C and in FORTRAN, functions can be passed as arguments. But in C, and not in FORTRAN, variables can be defined that point to functions. C function names are really (constant) pointers to functions. Function pointers offer flexibility to the programmer because they can be made to point to different functions (provided the functions have the same result type, number of arguments, and argument types).

Arguments in C are passed by value while arguments are passed by reference in FORTRAN. In other words, C parameters do not become synonyms for the corresponding arguments. Instead they become synonyms for temporary variables that contain the same value as the corresponding arguments. As a result, changing the value of a parameter does not change the value of the corresponding argument. Passing arguments by reference, as in FORTRAN, is simulated by passing pointers to the arguments.

If a C function is called before its definition is encountered, regardless of whether it is in the same source file (program unit) or in a different source file, then it must be declared. A function declaration is called a "function prototype" because it specifies not only the function result type, but also the parameter types. This facilitates better type checking. The compiler can check that the function is being called with the right number of the arguments that are of the correct type.

Unlike FORTRAN, C allows users to write functions that accept a variable number of arguments. Functions are discussed in detail in the next chapter.

6. STORAGE CLASSES

In C programs, the storage class of a variable determines its lifetime and scope. There are four storage classes: external, file static, automatic, and function static. To be precise, there is another storage class called *register*, but it is really a variant of the automatic storage class. The only C storage classes for which there is a direct counterpart in FORTRAN are the external and automatic storage classes.

The scope of an external variable is the set of files containing its definition and matching declarations, and its lifetime is the lifetime of the program. External variables are used for inter-function communication. These functions can be in the same file or in different files. External variable definitions are given outside the function body. One file must contain the definition of an external variable. Each of the other files, where this external variable is referenced, must contain a matching declaration. External variable declarations must be preceded by the keyword *extern*. External variable definitions, however, *must not* use the keyword *extern*. Function definitions (declarations) are automatically assumed to be external definitions (declarations).

As an example, consider an external integer variable *n* that is used for inter-file inter-function communication between functions *main* and *line*. Here is the file containing the definitions of variable *n* and function *main*, and the declaration of function *line*:

```
int n = 0;
char *line(void);
main(void)
{
    … n … line() …
}
```

Now here is the file that contains a matching external declaration for *n* and the definition of function *line*:

```
extern int n;
char *line(void)
{
    … n …
}
```

Had *main* and *line* been in the same file, then there would have been no need for the external declaration of *n* or for the declaration of *line* provided the definition of *line* was given before that of *main*:

```
int n = 0;

char *line(void)
{
    … n …
}

main(void)
{
    … n … line() …
}
```

The semantics of external variables can be easily implemented by using the blank *COMMON* facility of FORTRAN. Named *COMMON* can be used to limit visibility of external variables to specific program units.

File static variables are like external variables except that their scopes are restricted to the files that contain their definitions. These variables are used for communication between functions in the same file. File static variable definitions are given outside a function body and must be preceded by the keyword *static*.

For example, if the variable *n* shown above is to be used just for communication between functions contained in the same file, then its scope can be restricted to the file by defining it as a static variable:

```
static int n = 0;
```

Defining *n* as a file static variable ensures that functions in other files will not be able to access or update the value of *n*.

Although FORTRAN *COMMON* variables can be used for communication between subprograms in the same program unit, there is no way of restricting the scope of such variables to just one program unit.

The scope of an automatic variable is the function containing its definition and its lifetime is the lifetime of the function. By default, all variables declared inside functions have the automatic storage class. These variables are automatically allocated upon function entry and deallocated upon function exit. The compiler can be instructed to put automatic variables, if possible, in registers for fast access by preceding the variable definitions with the keyword *register*.

Function static variables are like file static variables except that they are defined inside a function and this restricts their scope to be the function body. Unlike automatic variables, function static variables are allocated once, at the beginning of the program, and they are not deallocated upon function exit. Function static variables are used to remember values across function calls. The FORTRAN *SAVE* statement can be used to get functionality equivalent to function static variables.

Now here is a summary of the scope and lifetime of variables of different storage classes. The scope of an external variable is the set of files containing its definition and the corresponding declarations, the scope of a file static variable is the file containing its definition, and the scope of an automatic or a function static variable is the function containing its definition. The lifetime of external and static variables is the same as the lifetime of the program and the lifetime of automatic variables is the lifetime of the function containing them.

The different variable scopes associated with the various storage classes allow a programmer to restrict the visibility of variables and functions to those parts of the program that need to access the variables and functions. The different lifetimes allow the storage to be allocated as and when needed.

7. SIGNAL HANDLING

Unlike FORTRAN, C provides facilities for catching signals (interrupts). Signal handling facilities extend the expressiveness of a language. These facilities are discussed in detail in Chapter 4.

8. EXERCISES

1. What are the advantages of initializing variables in their definitions instead of initializing them with assignment statements?

2. Suppose a is an array with n elements of type *complex* which is defined as

```
typedef struct{
    double r, i;
} complex;
```

Write a program to read values into this array and then determine the index of the element with the maximum value for the expression $r*r+i*i$, where r and i are components of the complex array element.

3. Write a FORTRAN version of the above C program. Compare the two programs.

CHAPTER 4

FUNCTIONS

Functions and files, like the subprograms and program units in FORTRAN, are the modularization facilities in C for partitioning programs into smaller components. Functions allow the executable part of a program to be partitioned into smaller components. And files are used to group together logically related functions, definitions, and declarations. Files in C, like the program units in FORTRAN, are the compilation units, i.e., they are the program components that can be independently compiled.

1. FUNCTION DEFINITIONS

By now, we have seen several examples of C function definitions. Here is the general form of function definitions:

result-type function-name (*parameter-declarations*)
{
    type declarations, variable definitions, & declarations
    statements
}

The first line of the function definition can be prefixed by the keyword *static* to restrict the scope of the function to the file containing it.

A function can have zero or more parameters. The part of the function enclosed within curly braces is called the *function body*. Variables defined inside a function body are called local variables, and their scope is limited to the function body. Like the scope of local variables, the scope of the function parameters is limited to the function body. In fact, function parameters are very much like local variables. Variables declared or defined outside a function body but in the same file as the function are called global variables and they can be referenced from within the function. The scope of an *external* global variable spans across multiple files while that of a *static* global variable is restricted to the file containing the variable definition. The scope of types declared within a function body is restricted to the function body; the scope of types declared outside the function body is restricted to the file containing the function body.

Parameterless functions are specified by giving the type *void* in place of the parameter declarations. Users can also define functions that accept a variable number of arguments. The header of such a function has a trailing ellipsis after the declaration of the fixed part of the parameter list. Definition of such functions, which cannot be declared in FORTRAN, will be discussed later.

Function definitions in ANSI C are different from those used in K&R C. Function definitions in K&R C are of the form

result-type function-name (*parameters*)
    parameter declarations
{
    type declarations, variable definitions, & declarations
    statements
}

If a function does not have any parameters, then the function name is followed by an empty pair of parentheses.

As an example illustrating the difference between ANSI and K&R C style function definitions, consider the following function (stored in file *msg.c*):

```
#include <stdio.h>
void msg(char *s)
{
    printf("%s\n", s);
}
```

This function would be defined in K&R C as (stored in file *msgkr.c*)

```
#include <stdio.h>
void msg(s)
    char *s;
{
    printf("%s\n", s);
}
```

ANSI C supports K&R C style function definitions. However, they should not be used because they are slated to go away at some future time.

1.1 MAIN FUNCTION & COMMAND-LINE ARGUMENTS

Each program must have a function named *main*. This is the function that is first called when a program starts executing. Arguments can be passed from the operating system (such as MS-DOS) command line to function *main*. The operating system calls *main* with two arguments: *argc*, which is the number of command-line arguments, and *argv*, which is an array of pointers to strings, each of which points to one command-line argument. The command name is always passed as the first argument, in string *argv*[*0*]. Consequently, the value of *argc* is always at least one.

As an example of a program that is called with command-line arguments, consider the following program that counts and prints the number of characters and lines in each file (stored in file *fcnt.c*):

```
/*count number of characters & lines in files*/
#include <stdio.h>
main(int argc, char *argv[])
{
    int i, nc, nl, c;
            /*nc = no of char, nl = no oflines*/
    FILE *fp;

    nc = nl = 0;
    for (i=1; i < argc; i++)
    {
        if ((fp=fopen(argv[i], "r")) == NULL) {
            printf("Invalid file %s\n",argv[i]);
            continue;
        }
        while ((c=getc(fp)) != EOF){
            if (c == '\n')
                nl++;
            nc++;
        }
        printf("%s:chars=%d,lines=%d\n",argv[i],nc,nl);
        fclose(fp);
    }
}
```

After the character and line counting program is compiled and linked to produce an executable file *fcnt*, it is invoked as

fcnt *file_1 file_2 ... file_n*

For example, the command

fcnt fcnt.c

counts the number of characters and lines in file *fcnt.c* which contains the C program shown above.

In FORTRAN, it is not possible to invoke programs with command-line arguments. Information passed as command-line arguments would have to be passed as input to the program.

2. FUNCTION PROTOTYPES (DECLARATIONS)

Either the definition of a function or its prototype (also called its declaration) must appear in a program before the function can be called. A function declaration must be given if the function definition is contained in another file, or if it appears after a call to the function.

Function prototypes are of the form

result-type   function-name   (parameter-types-or-declarations) ;

Here are some examples:

```
int get(int *p);
void print(node *root);
void add(node **, int);
```

Notice that parameter declarations are given in the prototypes of *get* and *print* while only parameter types are given in the prototype of *add*.

If a function does not have any parameters, then the type *void* is specified as the parameter type, e.g.,

```
int getchar(void);
```

If the number of arguments that a function will be called will vary with the call, then the variable arguments are specified by a trailing ellipsis. For example, the declaration

```
int max(int n, ...);
```

specifies that *max* will be called with at least one argument, its first argument, which will be of type *int*. The types or declarations of the variable arguments, which must be the trailing arguments, are not specified. The types however must be known a priori and they are used in the function body to access the arguments. Defining a function with a variable number of arguments is discussed later.

For C library functions, header files containing function prototypes are normally provided, and these files should be included instead of giving explicit function prototypes in files that contain calls to these functions.

A function prototype helps the compiler generate the correct code for the function result, allows it to ensure that the function is called with the right number of arguments of the right types, and to ensure that the function result is used correctly with respect to its type.

This checking is not possible in K&R C because neither the function parameters nor their types are given in the function declaration. For example, the functions whose prototypes were given above would be declared as

```
int get();
void print();
void add();
```

3. FUNCTION CALLS

Function calls are of the form

function-name (arguments)

As we have seen several times by now, functions calls can be used in expressions (assuming they return a value of a type other than *void*). A function that has no parameters is called without any arguments (nothing is specified to correspond to the *void* type in its prototype which specifies that the function is parameterless).

4. ARGUMENT PASSING

Function arguments are "passed by value" in C. This means that each argument is evaluated and its result copied to the corresponding parameter. Any changes to the parameter itself have no effect on the corresponding argument. Of course, if the parameter is a pointer and the corresponding argument is a pointer to a variable, then changing the value of the object pointed to by the parameter will, in effect, change the value of the variable. This is because both the parameter and the argument point to the same object, that is, the variable whose value is changed. To change a variable's value by calling a function, the address of the variable must be passed to the function.

In case of an array argument, the array is not copied in C. Instead, a pointer to the beginning of the array is copied to the parameter. This is because an array name is actually a pointer to the beginning of the array.

As an example illustrating the argument passing mechanism of C, we shall write a function *cube* that cubes its argument. Suppose we write the *cube* function as

```
void cube(double x)
{
    x = x*x*x;
}
```

cube, as written above, will not work correctly because, although it cubes its parameter *x*, it has no effect on the corresponding argument. Consider, for example, a call to *cube*:

```
cube(a);
```

As explained before, the argument *a* is copied into the parameter *x* which is then cubed. However, *a* is not cubed; in fact, nothing happens to *a*. We have two choices in modifying *cube* so that it does actually give us the cube of the argument supplied:

- *cube* can return as its result the cube of its argument which can then be assigned to the variable passed as the argument.

- *cube* can be given the address of the variable to be cubed; *cube* can use this address to cube the variable.

Here is the first solution:

```
double cube(double x)
{
    return x*x*x;
}
```

Here is how a variable will be cubed:

```
a = cube(a);
```

Now here is the second solution:

```
void cube(double *x)
{
    (*x) = (*x)*(*x)*(*x);
}
```

The address of the variable to be cubed is passed to *cube*:

```
cube(&a);
```

Let us now consider how to change the value of a pointer variable by calling a function. As discussed above, the address of the pointer variable (a pointer to the pointer), and not the pointer variable itself, must be given as an argument to the function in question. Suppose we want to write a function *alloc* that encapsulates the following storage allocation code:

```
#include <stdlib.h>
#include <stdio.h>
    ...
char *p;
int n;
    ...
if ((p = malloc(n)) != NULL) {
    puts("not enough heap storage\n");
    exit(1);
}
```

Here is one possible definition for function *alloc* (stored in file *alloc.c*):

```
#include <stdlib.h>
#include <stdio.h>
void alloc(char **pp, int n)
{
    if ((*pp = malloc(n)) != NULL) {
        puts("not enough heap storage\n");
        exit(1);
    }
}
```

Notice that the first parameter is a pointer to a character pointer and not just a character pointer. To set the character pointer *p* to point to *n* bytes of allocated storage, *alloc* will be called as

```
alloc(&p, n);
```

5. FUNCTION RESULT & COMPLETION

The value returned by a function, that is, the function result, is specified with the *return* statement which has the form

```
return e;
```

The type of expression *e* must match the function type (or it should be convertible to the function type according to the "usual arithmetic conversion" rules). The semantics of the FORTRAN and C *return* statements with a *return* expression are thus quite different.

Executing the *return* statement also completes execution of the function. Every function whose result type is not the *void* type must terminate by executing a *return* statement. Such a function must not terminate by just completing execution of the function body; otherwise, the value returned by the function will be garbage.

Functions with a *void* result type can complete execution by completing execution of the program body or by executing a *return* statement of the form

```
return;
```

A function can have several *return* statements.

6. RECURSION

C supports recursion; that is, C allows a function to call itself. Parameters are important, but not necessary, for writing effective recursive functions. The basic idea behind recursion is to decompose a problem into smaller subproblems which are solved by recursively calling the function that was called to solve the original problem. This approach, as mentioned earlier, is divide-and-conquer approach to problem solving. Recursion is an important programming tool because many algorithms are naturally recursive.

To illustrate recursion, we will implement a recursive version of the binary search example given in Chapter 2 (stored in file *rsearch.c*):

```
/*search sorted array a for value x; return*/
/*k such that a[k]==x; otherwise, return -1*/

int search(int a[], int l, int u, int x)
{
    int k;

    if (l > u)
        return -1;
    else if (a[k = (l+u)/2] == x)
        return k;
    else if (a[k] < x)
        search(a, k+1, u, x);
    else
        search(a, l, k-1, x);
}
```

Function *search* searches an ordered array *a* for an element with a value equal to *x*. It starts off by checking to see whether or not array *a* is a null array. Then *search* checks to see whether or not the middle element of *a* is equal to *x*. If yes, then the search is complete. Otherwise, depending upon whether the middle element of *a* is less than or greater than *x*, function *search* is called recursively to search either the upper or lower half of *a*.

Recursion does not come for free. There is a cost associated with it: the cost of the function call, passing the parameters, setting up the local variables and the function return. Recursion should be used only when it simplifies program understanding or makes the algorithm simple to implement.

In languages such as FORTRAN that do not provide appropriate facilities for writing recursive functions, programmers are unlikely to write recursive programs. Instead, they will implement recursive algorithms with iterative programs, i.e., with programs that use loops. This is more work for the programmer and it also makes the final program harder to understand because, unlike the algorithm it implements, the program will not be recursive. There will be no direct mapping from the algorithm to the program.

Recursive calls should be made conditionally, that is, only when some conditions are satisfied. If a recursive call is made unconditionally, that is, a function calls itself every time it is called, then the recursion will never end (the function will call itself again and again forever). Of course, a program containing such a function will eventually terminate (in an error state) by running out of storage. Note that a certain amount of storage has to be allocated for every function call. Among other things, this storage is used for the function arguments, for the automatic variables in the function, and for saving the address of the instruction to be executed after the function has completed execution.

7. STATIC VARIABLES

Local variables are, by default, automatic variables. They are automatically allocated afresh every time a function is called and deallocated when the function completes execution. Consequently, automatic variables do not retain values across function calls.

Local variables that are qualified with the storage class *static*, i.e., function static variables, retain their values across function calls. Global variables can also be used to do the same thing but, unlike local static variables, their scope is not restricted to a single function.

As an example illustrating the use of a local static variable, consider a multi-user operating system such as the UNIX system in which many users simultaneously share the same computer. The operating system executes each user's command for a fraction of a second (or some other time unit) before going on to the next user. This fraction is called a *time slice* and this strategy of sharing a computer between several users is called *time sharing*. If the computer is powerful enough, then time sharing will give each user the illusion that the user has a dedicated (single-user) computer. One way of picking the next user to get a time slice is to search an array called the *process table* (*user table*) which contains information about all user programs. To make sure that each user gets a time slice in turn, the process table is searched sequentially for the next user starting just after the position, in the process table, of the last user to get a time slice. A local static variable, say *lastuser*, is used to remember the index of the last user. The search for the next user is started with the index value *lastuser* + 1. Here is a function for picking the next user (stored in file *nextuser.c*):

```
extern int user[]; /*user table*/
extern int n;      /*table size*/

int nextuser(void)
{
    static lastuser = 0;

    while (1)
    {
        lastuser = ++lastuser % n;
        if (user[lastuser] != (-1))
          /*user[i] == -1 indicates empty slot*/
            return lastuser;
    }
}
```

Local static variables should be initialized in their definitions (the compiler will initialize them at compile time). Initialization with assignment statements is ineffective because, each time a function is called, these statements will be reexecuted thus destroying the previous values of the local static variables.

8. COMMUNICATION BETWEEN FUNCTIONS

In addition to communicating by means of parameters, functions can also communicate by using global variables. There are two kinds of global variables: *file static* and *external* variables. File static variables are used for communicating between functions in the same file (the scope of static global variables is restricted to the file containing them). External variables can be used to communicate between any two functions in a program even though they may be in different files.

To illustrate the use of a file static variable, we will give the skeleton code for implementing a pseudo-random number generator. The random number generator consists of two functions: *newseed* and *random*. Function *newseed* is called to set the random number seed, that is, the initial value used for generating the random number sequence. Function *random* returns the next random number (between 0 and 9 in our example). Here are the two random generator functions which are stored in the same file:

```
static int seed = 0;

void newseed(int i)
{
    seed = i;
}

int random(void)
{
    seed = compute random number using seed;
    return seed % 10;
            /*random number between 0 & 9*/
}
```

We have not shown you the code for generating the random number. Generating "good" random number sequences is not easy. The reader interested in learning more about random numbers is referred to the classic *The Art of Computer Programming* (Volume 2) by D. E. Knuth [Knut69].

External variables are used primarily for communication between functions stored in different files. For each external variable, one file must contain its definition and each of the other files must contain a matching declaration. By default, a variable definition given outside a function is an external definition. The presence of the keyword *extern* distinguishes an external declaration from an external definition.

Suppose that the above random number generation functions are stored in separate files. Then if variable *seed* is to be accessible to both functions, it will have to be defined as an external variable. Here is the file containing the definition of the external variable *seed* and the definition of function *newseed*:

```
int seed = 0;

void newseed(int i)
{
    seed = i;
}
```

An initial value for an external variable can only be given in its definition but not in its declaration.

Here is the file containing a matching declaration of the external variable *seed* and the definition of function *random*:

```
extern int seed;

int random(void)
{
    seed =   compute random number using seed;
    return seed % 10;
                /*random number between 0 & 9*/
}
```

9. FUNCTION NAMES AS ARGUMENTS

A function can be passed as an argument to other functions by just giving the function name as an argument. A function name is really a constant pointer to the code for executing the function. As an example, suppose we want to write a function *printrange* (stored in file *printrng.c*) that prints the values of a function argument between the specified limits *a* and *b* using an interval equal to *step*:

```
#include <stdio.h>
void printrange(double (*pf)(double), double a,
                double b, double step, char *fname)
{
    double x;

    for (x = a; x <= b; x += step)
        printf("%s(%g) = %g\n",fname,x,(*pf)(x));
}
```

Here is an example use of this function:

```
void printrange(double (*pf)(double), double a,
                double b, double step, char *fname);

double dbl(double x)   /*returns 2*x*/
{
    return 2*x;
}

main(void)
{
    double a = 1, b = 10, step = 1;
    printrange(dbl, a, b, step, "dbl");
}
```

Because function *dbl* was defined before it was used, it was not necessary to declare it. Had its definition been given after that of function *main*, then it would have been necessary to declare it:

```
void printrange(double (*pf)(double), double a,
                double b, double step, char *fname);
main(void)
{
    double dbl(double), a = 1, b = 10, step = 1;
    printrange(dbl, a, b, step, "dbl");
}

double dbl(double x)   /* returns 2*x */
{
    return 2*x;
}
```

Here is the output of the above program:

```
dbl(1)  = 2
dbl(2)  = 4
dbl(3)  = 6
dbl(4)  = 8
dbl(5)  = 10
dbl(6)  = 12
dbl(7)  = 14
dbl(8)  = 16
dbl(9)  = 18
dbl(10) = 20
```

10. VARIABLE NUMBER OF ARGUMENTS

Many of FORTRAN's intrinsic functions accept a variable number of arguments, but FORTRAN does not provide facilities for writing such functions. However, C does provide such facilities. I will illustrate these facilities by showing you how to write a function *max* (similar to the one in FORTRAN) that computes the maximum value of a variable number of integer arguments. *max* takes $n+1$ arguments: an integer specifying the number of arguments of which the maximum is to be computed, and the *n* arguments themselves.

The variable argument list is specified with an ellipsis in the function header (and in the function prototype). Variable arguments are accessed by using the pre-defined type *va_list*, the macros *va_start* and *va_arg*, and the function *va_end*. Header file *stdarg.h* contains the appropriate definitions and/or declarations of these items.

Here is the program:

```c
#include <stdarg.h>
#include <stdio.h>
int max(int n, ...)
{
    int k, m, temp;
    va_list args;

    va_start(args, n);
    switch (n) {
    case 0:
        fprintf(stderr, "max: error, first arg = 0");
        exit(0);
    case 1:
        m = va_arg(args, int);
        va_end(args);
        return m;
    default:
        m = va_arg(args, int);
        break;
    }
    for (k = 1; k < n; k++)
        m = (temp = va_arg(args, int)) > m ? temp : m;

    va_end(args);
    return m;
}
```

To access the variable arguments, a variable of type *va_list*, i.e., *args*, is first declared. Then the variable argument access initialization routine *va_start* is called with two arguments: *args* and the last parameter before the ellipsis, which is *n* in this case. The variable arguments are stored in *args*. Each successive argument of the variable arguments is accessed by calling macro *va_arg* with *args* and the appropriate variable argument type. All the variable arguments in this example are of type *int*. Finally, after all the variable arguments have been accessed, the function *va_end* is called.

11. INDEPENDENT COMPILATION

Line FORTRAN compilers, C compilers support independent compilation, that is, they allow parts of a program to be compiled independently of each other. The unit of compilation of a C program is the file. Large programs should be partitioned into several files for ease of manipulation and compilation. If this is done, then when the program is modified, only the files that have been affected by the modification will need to be recompiled. The whole program need not be recompiled. Compiling an entire program every time it is modified, especially if the program is large, can be very time consuming.

To produce an executable version of a program, each file containing parts of the program is compiled to produce an object file. These object files are then linked together, with appropriate libraries, such as the standard and math libraries, to produce an executable version of the program.

As far as possible, programs should be designed as collections of small functions. Related definitions, declarations, and function bodies should be stored in the same file, but to minimize the recompilation effort, the files should be kept as small as possible.

For details about how to invoke the compiler and linker, please refer to your C compiler manual.

12. INTERRUPT (SIGNAL) HANDLING

Unlike FORTRAN, C provides facilities for catching or handling signals (interrupts). Signal handling facilities extend the expressiveness of a language.

Signals are generated in C programs in two ways:

1. Program errors resulting in situations such as a zero divide or an overflow.

2. Interaction from the program environment, e.g., the user typing the control-C character to terminate an application.

When a signal is raised, execution is transferred to the corresponding signal handler function, if any. Otherwise, default signal handling takes place which can in some cases mean program termination.

12.1 STANDARD SIGNALS

ANSI C defines the following standard signals:

signal name	explanation
SIGABRT	raised by calling function *abort*.
SIGFPE	floating-point error
SIGILL	illegal instruction execution attempt
SIGINT	interrupt
SIGSEGV	illegal memory reference
SIGTERM	terminate (from the environment)

Note that *SIGINT* is raised whenever the user types control-C or control-break.

C compilers may support other non-standard signals. See your C compiler reference manual for details about non-standard signals and the conditions under which signals are raised.

12.2 SPECIFYING A SIGNAL HANDLER

To set up a signal handler (an interrupt trap), function *signal* is called with two arguments: the signal (interrupt type) *sig*, and the name of the signal handler (trap) function *f* which is to be invoked when this signal is trapped. As its result, function *signal* returns the previous trap function for the specified signal.

User-defined signal handling functions must accept one *int* argument (the signal number) and must have the result type *void*. The signal number corresponds to the value of the signal name (listed in the table above).

There are two special interrupt handling functions: *SIG_IGN* which specifies that the signal is to be ignored and *SIG_DFL* which specifies that default action is to be taken when the signal is caught.

Function *signal* is often used in conjunction with the *setjmp* macro and the *longjmp* function. Macro *setjmp* records the program state (e.g., the program counter) in a buffer and function *longjmp* is used to restore the program state. See the Appendix for more details about these routines.

12.3 RAISING SIGNALS

Typically, signals are raised automatically and a program just provides signal handlers. But signals can also be explicitly raised in a program by calling function *raise*. However, this is rarely done.

12.4 HANDLING SIGNALS

When a signal is raised, execution transfers to the signal handler, if one has been specified. Otherwise, default action is taken as specified by the C implementation. This action may be to ignore the signal, to terminate the program, or to respond to the signal. Upon completion of the handler, program execution is resumed at the point of interruption. Unless appropriate action has been taken in the handler to respond to the cause of the signal (if this is necessary), returning from the handler may cause the signal to be raised again.

12.5 SIGNAL HANDLING EXAMPLE

Consider the following program (stored in file *signal.c*) that prints the positive numbers starting from 0. The user can terminate the program anytime by typing control-C and then answering affirmatively to the program's query; a negative response will cause the program to continue printing:

```
#include <signal.h>
#include <stdio.h>

void quit(int sig)
{
    int c;
    printf("you really want to quit? (y or n):");
    if ((c = getchar()) == 'y' || c == 'Y')
        exit(0);
    while (getchar() != '\n');
    signal(SIGINT, quit);
}
main()
{
    int i;

    signal(SIGINT, quit);
    for(i=0; ; i++)
        printf("%d\n", i);
}
```

Function *signal* is first called in *main* to set up the signal handler function *quit* and then again, if necessary, in *quit* itself to reset the signal trapping.

13. PROGRAM TERMINATION

C programs can terminate in three different ways: by completing execution of the *main* function, by calling the *exit* function, or by executing the *return* statement in the *main* function. Function *exit* closes all open files. It also cleans the output buffers causing the buffered items to be written to the appropriate files. *exit* is called with a zero argument to indicate successful (normal) termination and with a non-zero argument to indicate error (abnormal) termination. This function is called automatically when a program terminates by completing execution of the *main* function or by executing the *return* statement in the *main* function. In this case, the argument of *exit* is unspecified.

14. ACCESSING OPERATING SYSTEM FACILITIES

Unlike FORTRAN, C provides the library function, *system*, which can be used to execute any command of the underlying operating system. For example, the calls

```
system("cls"); system("show 1");
```

will clear the screen by executing the MS-DOS command "cls" and then run the user program *show* with the argument 1. Note that a complete path name specifying the command to be executed can also be given as an argument to *system*. The *system* command returns -1 if the specified command could not be executed.

15. CALLING ROUTINES WRITTEN IN OTHER LANGUAGES

Most C compilers provide (non-standard) facilities for calling routines written in high-level languages such as FORTRAN and Pascal. Machine language functions can also be called from C programs. Calling such functions is just like calling ordinary C functions. Of course, for a machine language function to be called from a C program, it must be written according to the conventions used by the C compiler. For example, machine language functions must follow the C compiler's convention for storing the arguments and the return address on the stack. Details of these conventions should be in the manual describing the C compiler. (Note that your C compiler may also provide an option instructing it to generate assembly language code. You may be able to use the assembly code generated for a C function to determine the conventions used by your C compiler and then pattern the machine language function on this code.)

16. EXAMPLES

16.1 A GENERAL PURPOSE SWAP ROUTINE

Consider the problem of writing a function *swap* that exchanges the values of two variables of any type including derived types such as arrays and structures. There are two problems that must be solved:

- C function argument types must match the parameter types. So how can arguments of arbitrary types be passed to the *swap* function?

- Arguments to be exchanged will be of different sizes depending upon their type and, in case of arrays, the number of array dimensions and their sizes. How do we know how many elements of an array to swap? In other words, how do we determine the argument size?

The first problem is solved by defining *swap* to accept character pointers specifying the addresses of the objects to be swapped; this requires that the user convert the object addresses to character pointers when calling *swap*. The second problem is solved by incorporating a third argument that specifies the argument size.

Here is the general *swap* function:

```
void swap(char *a, char *b, int n)
{
    char tmp;

    while(n-- >0) {
        tmp = *(a+n);
        *(a+n) = *(b+n);
        *(b+n) = tmp;
    }
}
```

Pointers *a* and *b* must refer to the beginning of the objects to be swapped.

Here are some variable definitions and some sample calls to *swap*:

```
typedef struct {
    char *name[MAX];
    int age;
} employee;

employee a, b;
char x[MAX], y[MAX];
char *s, *t;
    ...
swap((char *)&s, (char *)&t, sizeof(char *));
swap(x, y, MAX);
swap((char *) &a, (char *) &b, sizeof(employee));
```

Strings implemented as pointers can be swapped by just exchanging the values of the pointers. Alternatively, instead of swapping pointer values, elements of the two strings can be physically exchanged:

```
swap(s, t, MAX);
```

Unlike arrays implemented using pointers, explicitly defined arrays cannot be swapped by just exchanging pointer values because array names are constant pointers whose values cannot be changed.

16.2 SORTING

Sorting is probably the single most important computer activity. Consequently, it is important to design efficient sorting routines. We will show you two different sorting programs: bubble sort and shell sort. Shell sort is a variation of bubble or interchange sort that, on the average, performs much better than bubble sort.

Bubble sort works as follows: assume that the left part of array *a*, up to and including element *a*[*i*], has been sorted. (Initially, the sorted part of the array consists of only element *a*[*0*].) Element *a*[*i+1*], whose value is *x*, is now interchanged with adjacent elements on the left until the left part of the array up to and including element *a*[*i+1*], whose value may now not be *x*, are in order. This process is repeated until the whole array is sorted.

Here is function *bubble* (stored in file *bubble.c*) that sorts an array of integers in increasing order:

```
void sort(int a[], int n)
{
    int i, j, tmp;

    for (i=1; i<n; i++)
        for (j=i-1; j>=0 && a[j]>a[j+1]; j--) {
            tmp = a[j];
            a[j] = a[j+1];
            a[j+1] = tmp;
        }
}
```

Bubble sort is not very efficient because every time the left part of the array is to be extended with a new element a large number of interchanges are required on the average to shift the new element into position. Shell sort orders the array in several passes. In the first pass, instead of comparing adjacent elements, it compares and exchanges elements separated by d-1 elements. With each successive pass, d is reduced until eventually, for the last pass, it equals 1 (i.e., adjacent elements are compared and exchanged). The idea is that elements that are grossly out of position will be interchanged in the earlier passes which do not require so many interchanges. The last pass is exactly like bubble sort, but the hope is that very few elements will need to be interchanged in the last pass.

Here is function *shellsort* (stored in *shell.c*) that sorts an array of integers in increasing order [Kern78]:

```
void shellsort(int a[], int n)
{
    int i, j, tmp, d;

    for (d = n/2; d>0; d = d/2)
        for (i=d; i<n; i++)
            for (j=i-d; j>=0&&a[j]>a[j+d]; j=j-d){
                tmp = a[j];
                a[j] = a[j+d];
                a[j+d] = tmp;
            }
}
```

16.3 QUEUES

A *queue* is a data structure which is used to implement the first-in-first-out (FIFO) discipline. The first element inserted into a queue is the first element that will be removed from the queue. Here are functions for interfacing with a queue of integers:

empty() If the queue is empty, return non-zero; otherwise, zero.

full()   If the queue is full, return non-zero; otherwise, zero.

add(x)   Add element x to the queue. If successful, return non-zero; otherwise, zero.

get(p)   Store the first element of the queue in *p. This element is then removed from the queue. If successful, return non-zero; otherwise, zero.

Now here are the prototypes of the functions implementing the queue data structure (stored in file *queue.h*):

```
int empty(void), full(void), add(int x), get(int *p);
```

Here are the definitions of variables and of functions implementing the queue data structure (stored in file *queue.c*):

```
#include "queue.h"

#define N 128
static int a[N], in = 0, out = 0, n = 0;

int empty(void) {return n == 0;}
int full(void)  {return n == N;}

int add(int x)
{
    if (full())
        return 0;
    a[in] = x; in = (in+1) % N;
    n++;
    return 1;
}

int get(int *p)
{
    if (empty())
        return 0;
    *p = a[in]; out = (out+1) % N;
    n--;
    return 1;
}
```

Notice the use of static global variables for communication between functions.

16.4 PAGINATOR

As another example illustrating how command-line arguments are given to a C program, we will write a paginator program, that is, a program that displays a file on the screen one page at a time. The file to be displayed with the pagination program, called *pager*, is supplied as an argument:

pager *file*

By default, *pager* assumes the page length to be 24 lines. An alternative page length can be supplied as the second command-line argument when invoking *pager*:

pager *file page-length*

Here is the *pager* program (stored in file *pager.c*):

```
#include <stdio.h>
#define LL 132
#define PL 24

/*page length can be supplied as the second*/
/*argument on the command line*/
main(int argc, char *argv[])
{
   char line[LL+1];
   int n, pl = PL;
   FILE *fp;

   if ((fp = fopen(argv[1], "r")) == NULL) {
     printf("error, cannot open file %s\n",argv[1]);
     exit(1);
   }
   if (argc == 3)
     sscanf(argv[2], "%d", &pl);

   n = 0;
   while (fgets(line, LL, fp) != NULL) {
     if (n++ < pl)
       printf("%s", line);
     else {
       printf("\033[7mType enter for more:\033[0m");
       while (getchar() != '\n')
         ;
       printf("%s", line);
       n = 1;
     }
   }
   fclose(fp);
}
```

17. EXERCISES

1. Implement the queue functions (of example 16.3) without using global variables. Compare the two solutions.

2. Compare the efficiency of bubble sort and shell sort by analyzing the number of comparisons and exchanges required to sort large samples of data. Modify the bubble and shell sort programs to count the comparisons and exchanges.

3. Write a general sorting routine *gsort* that can sort arrays with any type of elements. Function *gsort* will be called with the following arguments:

    a. A pointer to the first element of the array (of type *char **).

b. Number of elements in the array.
c. Size of the array elements.
d. Pointer to a function for comparing two array elements.

Suppose the array elements are of type *employee*:

```
typedef struct {
    char *name;
    int id;
} employee;
```

The comparison function for sorting the array according to employee id may then be written as

```
int lt(void *a, void *b)   /*a less than b*/
{
    employee *p = a, *q = b;

    return p->id < q->id ? 1 : 0;
}
```

CHAPTER 5

POINTERS

Pointers are used to directly access memory locations (a pointer value is a memory address). Only meaningful or valid pointer values should be used to access memory. Otherwise, you will get garbage when reading memory, and by writing to these addresses, you may destroy the program or the program data, or you may update the system information causing the operating system to crash. Valid pointer values are those that refer to dynamically allocated storage, and when allowed, addresses of variables and memory locations reserved for hardware devices. Some computer systems do not allow users to access all parts of memory. For example, the region of memory containing the operating system code and data may be out of bounds for users. Attempts to access invalid or prohibited addresses can cause program termination. Accessing memory using a null pointer value can also cause program termination.

Although pointers are a very powerful programming tool, it is relatively easy to make errors when using them. Consequently, pointers are a source of many programming errors, and they should therefore be used with great care. This is especially important because errors caused by pointers are hard to discover for their effects do not become apparent until long after the errors have occurred.

1. VOID POINTERS

Pointers of type *void*, i.e.,

```
void *
```

are special types of pointers. They are called *generic* pointers because they can be used in places where a pointer is expected regardless of the pointer type expected. Void pointers are automatically coerced to pointers of the right type. Void pointers are often used to

a. define variables that will hold values of different pointer types,

b. declare parameters that will be passed different types of argument pointers, and

c. specify the result type of a function that returns a pointer whose type will be implicitly or explicitly specified by the caller.

2. ALLOCATING & DEALLOCATING STORAGE

Objects can be freely created and referenced at run time by allocating an appropriate amount of storage, assigning the address of the storage to a pointer variable, and then referencing the object with the pointer. The only limitation on the number of objects that can be created at run time is the total amount of available memory.

Storage is allocated from an area of memory, called the *heap*, which is reserved for allocating storage for run-time (dynamic) objects. C provides a set of functions for allocating storage from the heap and freeing (deallocating) storage, that is, returning previously allocated storage to the heap.

Here is a brief description of the C storage allocation and deallocation functions:

malloc(n)	Allocate *n* bytes of storage. If successful, *malloc* returns a pointer, of type *void*, to the allocated storage. Otherwise, *malloc* returns the null pointer *NULL*. *malloc* is the storage allocation function that is used most often.
calloc(nelem, elemsize)	Allocate *nelem*elemsize* bytes of storage. *calloc* is like *malloc* but it sets all the bits of the allocated storage to zero.
realloc(ptr, n)	Change the size of a previously allocated storage region that begins at address *ptr* to *n* while ensuring that the storage contents are preserved. If necessary, a new block of memory is allocated; in this case the contents of the old memory block specified by *ptr* are copied to the new memory block, and the old memory block is deallocated. *realloc* returns a pointer to the (possibly new) *n*-byte block of memory. If reallocation is not possible, then *realloc* returns *NULL*.
free(ptr)	Free (deallocate) previously allocated storage that begins at the address specified by *ptr* and returns this storage to the heap. *free* returns 0 if it is successful; otherwise, it returns -1.

The above storage allocation functions are often collectively referred to as "storage allocators." The prototypes of the storage allocation and deallocation functions are stored in the header file *stdlib.h*. See the Appendix for a detailed description of these functions.

Here is an example of a commonly used programming paradigm for allocating storage using *malloc*:

```
#include <stddef.h>   /*contains defn. of NULL*/
#include <stdlib.h>
employee *pe;
    ...
if ((pe = malloc(sizeof(employee))) == NULL) {
    print error message and/or perform error action
}
```

As shown above, when using a storage allocator it is important to check whether or not the storage requested was allocated. The *sizeof* operator is frequently used in specifying the amount of storage required.

3. POINTER ARITHMETIC

C allows you to add an integer to and subtract an integer from a pointer, and subtract one pointer from another. However, other arithmetic operations on pointers, such as adding or multiplying two pointers, are not allowed. The effect of adding an integer i to a pointer p that points to objects of type T is to add the value $i*sizeof(T)$ to p; that is, the value added is the number of bytes occupied by i objects of type T. To add the integer value i, and not the space occupied by i objects of type T, casts must be used, for example,

```
p = (T *) ((int) p + i);
```

Similarly, the effect of subtracting an integer i from a pointer p, which points to objects of type T, is to subtract the value $i*sizeof(T)$ from p.

When subtracting one pointer from another, say p from q, both pointers being of the same type T, then the result is the number of items of type T that can be fitted in the memory between p and q. The result can be converted to bytes by multiplying it by $sizeof(T)$.

4. LISTS: AN EXAMPLE OF POINTER USE

After arrays, lists are probably the most important data structures in programming. In fact, there are languages like LISP which are built with the list type, and not the array type like in FORTRAN, as the primary data structure. Lists are typically implemented in C by using pointers. A pointer to the first element of the list is always kept. This pointer, called the *list head*, is used for accessing the list. A null list head, by convention, indicates that the list is empty.

Each element of the list is implemented with a structure that conceptually consists of two parts: the first part is a set of components for storing information, and the second part is a pointer that points to the next element in the list. A null pointer value signals the end of the list.

Lists of the type described above are called *singly-linked* lists because there is only one pointer (link) from one element to the next. Using this pointer, the list can be traversed in one direction: you can go from one list element to the next element but not to the previous element. Other types of lists, such as *doubly-linked* lists, allow list traversal in both directions: forward to the next element and back to the previous element. In doubly-linked lists two pointers must be kept: one for the next element and one for the previous element.

Building lists is straightforward. You start with the list head and insert a new element at an appropriate place in the list, e.g., you can insert it at the beginning of the list, in the middle of the list, or at the end of the list. Before showing you the code to do this, here are some declarations and definitions that we will use:

```
typedef struct elem {
    char name[MAX];
    struct elem *next;
} elem;

elem *h = NULL, *p;   /*h is the list head*/
                      /*p is a temporary ptr*/
char name[MAX];
```

Here is some code to allocate an element, assign values to it and insert it at the beginning of the list pointed to by *h*:

```
if ((p = malloc(sizeof(elem))) == NULL) {
    puts("not enough heap storage");
    exit(1);
}
strcpy(p->name, name);
p->next = h;
h = p;
```

The last two instructions are the ones which actually insert the element pointed by *p* in the list pointed by *h*. These two instructions should usually be encapsulated in a function, such as *add*, which can be called, for example, as *add(&h, p)*. Notice that the address of *h*, not its value, must be passed to *add* because function *add* may change the value of *h*. Here is the definition of function *add*:

```
void add(elem **h, *p)
{
    p->next = *h;
    *h = p;
}
```

Encapsulating the code for list insertion in a function such as *add* will facilitate making changes to the insertion strategy. Only the definition of this function may need to be changed instead of all the places where an element is inserted in a list.

Processing list elements, for example, printing all the list elements, requires stepping through the list sequentially one element at a time. Here is code for printing all the list elements:

```
for(p = h; p != NULL; p = p->next)
    printf("%s\n", p->name);
```

Unlike an array, a list is a sequential data structure. An arbitrary element of an array can be accessed with its subscript but accessing an arbitrary list element requires starting from the list head. For example, accessing the last element of a list requires starting with the list head and stepping, using the pointer to the next list element, through all the list elements. Lists also require more storage than arrays. Unlike arrays, lists need to keep pointers for list traversal. The extra storage required for singly-linked lists is one word (that is, the size of a pointer) per list element.

Having mentioned some disadvantages of lists, it is now time to mention some advantages of lists. Unlike arrays, lists can grow in size dynamically until you run out of storage. In many languages, including FORTRAN, the array size is fixed; once the array has been allocated, its size cannot be changed. Note that C is one of the few languages in which an array size can be changed, by using the function *realloc*, provided the array is implemented using pointers and using dynamically allocated storage. However, increasing the array size may require copying the existing array elements into a new region of memory. This array copying can be an expensive proposition, especially if the array involved is large and if it is done often.

Unlike in case of an array, items can be inserted between any two list elements without requiring shifting of the adjacent elements, and any element can be deleted without creating a gap in the list. Inserting an item into a list or deleting an item from a list requires only a few operations.

If a list is initially sorted, then this ordering of the list elements can be preserved if every new element is added between an appropriate pair of list elements. For example, when inserting a new element in a list that is sorted in increasing order, the new element should be added after an element less than or equal to the new element, but before an element greater than it. Lists can also be implemented with arrays by using subscripts to simulate pointers. However, such lists will not be as flexible as lists implemented using pointers. For example, in many languages it may not be possible to make the lists grow beyond the initial size of the array. This is not a problem in C, because as mentioned above, array sizes can be increased dynamically.

5. POINTERS & ARRAYS

In C there is a very strong relationship between pointers and arrays (and therefore strings). Arrays can be treated as pointers and vice versa. In many ways, arrays are primarily a convenient mechanism for manipulating pointers. Suppose a is declared as a character array. Then the ith element of array a is accessed using the array element notation $a[i]$. An array name is also a pointer to the first element of the array. For example, the array name a can be thought of as a character pointer that points to the first element of a, that is, it points to the beginning of the storage allocated for a. Hence, the ith element of a can also be accessed as $*(a+i)$. Similarly, any pointer value can be thought of as the name of an array that begins at the address specified by the pointer value. As an example, suppose that p is a character pointer that has been initialized properly. Then the ith byte of storage, relative to the address pointed to by i, can be referenced as $p[i]$. In general, if p is a pointer of type T, then $p[i]$ refers to the ith block of storage of size $sizeof(T)$ beginning from p.

Because array elements can be accessed using pointers and the storage referenced by a pointer can be accessed as array elements, C has no way of knowing whether or not a user is referring to a valid array element. Consequently, unlike FORTRAN, the C run-time system will not give a "subscript-out-of-range" error when an invalid array element is referenced, i.e., when a negative array subscript or a positive subscript greater than the upper array bound is encountered. A C array (or pointer) can, in effect, be used to access any element of accessible memory.

Strictly speaking, C can flag a subscript error for array elements accessed using the array subscript notation. One reason why C compilers do not check for invalid array subscripts is that array subscript checking is expensive. In general, it must be done at run time and this slows program execution. Recognizing the importance of subscript checking, at least in the program debugging phase, some C debugging tools such as C interpreters now check for invalid subscripts.

To illustrate the close relationship between arrays and pointers, we will write a pointer version of the function *left* that returns an n-character prefix of a string. The array version of *left*, which was given in Chapter 2, is shown below for your convenience:

```
#include <stdlib.h> /*decl. of exit*/
#include <stdio.h>
#include <string.h>
void left(char d[], char s[], int n)
          /*set d to the leftmost n*/
          /*characters of s          */
{
    if (n < 0 ) {
        fprintf(stderr, "error, n is negative\n");
        exit(1);
    }
    if (n > strlen(s))
        n = strlen(s);
    strncpy(d, s, n);
    d[n] = '\0';
}
```

Now here is the equivalent pointer version (stored in file *leftp.c*):

```
#include <stdio.h>
#include <string.h>
#include <stdlib.h>
void left(char *d, char *s, int n)
            /*set d to the leftmost n*/
            /*characters of s        */
{
    if (n < 0 ) {
        fprintf(stderr, "error, n is negative\n");
        exit(1);
    }
    if (n > strlen(s))
        n = strlen(s);
    strncpy(d, s, n);
    *(d+n) = '\0';
}
```

There is one difference between array names and pointers. An array name is a constant; its value cannot be changed. On the other hand, a pointer name is a variable whose value can be changed. As an example illustrating this difference, consider two strings defined as

```
char s[MAX], t[MAX];
```

whose values we want to exchange by calling function *swaps*:

```
void swaps(char **a, char **b)
{
    char *tmp;

    tmp = *a; *a = *b; *b = tmp;
}
```

Function *swaps* takes two pointers, of type pointer to character, as arguments and exchanges the strings pointed to by them. Calling *swaps* with the addresses of pointers *s* and *t*, which are character pointers, as in

```
swaps(&s, &t);  /*&s and &t are pointers to*/
                /*character pointers*/
```

is illegal because *s* and *t* are constants and extracting the address of a constant is not allowed. (Your C compiler may allow this but you will most likely get garbage). On the other hand, suppose *s* and *t* had been defined as character pointers and storage allocated for them dynamically, as shown below, by calling a storage allocator such as *malloc*. Then the call *swaps(&s, &t)* would be legal and it would exchange the values of the *s* and *t*:

```
char *s, *t;
    ...

if ((s = malloc(MAX)) == NULL) {
    fprintf(stderr, "not enough heap storage\n");
    exit(1);
}
if ((t = malloc(MAX)) == NULL) {
    fprintf(stderr, "not enough heap storage\n");
    exit(1);
}
    ...
swaps(&s, &t);
```

Of course, an alternative version of *swaps* that exchanges the two strings by swapping individual characters can be used with strings implemented by using explicitly defined arrays. However, in general, this will be relatively inefficient because it will require many more exchanges than just exchanging the pointer values as shown above.

6. DYNAMIC ARRAYS

C does not provide an explicit mechanism for specifying *dynamic arrays*, that is, arrays whose sizes can be specified at run time. However, dynamic arrays can easily be implemented in C by using pointers. Allocating a dynamic array is a two-step process: first a pointer variable is defined and then it is set to point to explicitly allocated storage. Remember that array names are really pointers (of type pointer to array element type). As an example, suppose we want to allocate an n-element integer array, where n is an arbitrary expression such as a parameter value. Using the storage allocator *malloc*, storage of size $n*sizeof(int)$ is allocated and its address assigned to a:

```
int *a;
    ...
if ((a = malloc(n * sizeof(int))) == NULL) {
    fprintf(stderr, "not enough heap storage\n");
    exit(1);
}
```

Function *malloc* takes as its argument the number of bytes to be allocated, which in our case is n times the size of each array element. It returns a pointer of type *void* which points to the block of storage allocated by it. The *void* pointer can be assigned to a pointer of any type.

Now this dynamic array with the name a can be used just like an explicitly defined array; for instance, you can reference element i of array a as $a[i]$.

Allocating 2-dimensional arrays is similar. The storage must be allocated for the total number of elements in the array and the array elements are referenced using the standard notation, for example, $p[i][j]$, where p is the pointer that points to the beginning of the allocated storage.

6.1 DEALLOCATING (ERASING) ARRAYS

Arrays implemented by using pointers and explicitly allocated storage can be deallocated (erased), that is, the storage used for these arrays can be freed by calling function *free*. The freed storage will be automatically reused by the storage allocation functions. Note that just assigning a new value to a pointer without explicitly freeing the storage pointed to by it may mean that this storage will be lost for the duration of the program.

7. EXAMPLES

7.1 DETERMINING THE AMOUNT OF STORAGE AVAILABLE FOR DYNAMIC ALLOCATION

Here is a program that determines the amount of storage that can be dynamically allocated, that is the size of the heap (stored in file *memsize.c*):

```
#include <stdio.h>
#include <stdlib.h>
#define N 1024   /*1 Kilobyte*/
main(void)
{
    int n = 0;

    while (malloc(N) != NULL)
        n++;
    printf("Dynamic Storage = %d Kbytes\n", n);
}
```

The size of the heap depends upon the hardware configuration, the size of the operating system, and the size of the program.

7.2 USING LISTS TO MANIPULATE STUDENT RECORDS

In this example, we will write a set of functions to implement and manipulate a list of student records. Each student record contains the student's name, id, and grade point average. Student records are kept in a file, ordered by student id. For fast interaction, the records are read into memory and stored, ordered by student id, in a list. The ordering of the student records is preserved in the presence of any additions to and deletions from the list. After the list updates have been completed, the student records are written, ordered by student id, back to the file.

The following list manipulation functions are to be implemented:

readlist(db, ps)   Read student records from the file *db* into a list whose header is stored in pointer *ps*; if successful, *readlist* returns 1; otherwise, 0.

writelist(*db, ps*)   Store the student records from the list pointed to by *ps*, maintaining the order in which they appear in the list, in the file *db*. If successful, *writelist* returns 1; otherwise, 0.

add(*ps, p*)   Add the student record pointed to by *p* to the list pointed to by *ps*. The list must remain ordered by student id. If successful, *add* returns 1; otherwise, 0.

remove(*ps, id*)   Remove from the list pointed to by *ps*, the student record with identification number *id*, if there is such a record; otherwise, do nothing.

in(*ps, id*)   Check to see whether or not a student record with identification number *id* is in the list pointed to by *ps*. If such a record is present, then *in* returns a pointer to this record; otherwise, *NULL*.

The following definitions and declarations, kept in the header file *student.h*, will be used by the student list functions:

```
#include <stdio.h>
#include <string.h>
#include <stdlib.h>

#define NAMELEN 32
#define STDSIZE (int) sizeof(student)

typedef struct student {
    char first, last[NAMELEN];
    int id;
    float gpa;
    struct student *next;
} student;

student *in(student *ps, int id);
int add(student **ps, student *p);
int readlist(char *db, student **ps);
int writelist(char *db, student *ps);
void remove(student **ps, int id);
```

Here is the definition of function *readlist* (stored in file *stread.c*):

```c
#include "student.h"
int readlist(char *db, student **ps)
{
    student *p, *last;
    FILE *fp;
    int none = 1;

    *ps = NULL;
    if ((fp = fopen(db,"r")) == NULL) {
        printf("cannot open file %s\n", db);
        return 0;
    }
    if ((p = malloc(STDSIZE)) == NULL){
        puts("not enough heap storage\n");
        fclose(fp);
        return 0;
    }
    while(fread((char *) p,STDSIZE,1,fp)==1){
        if (none)
            {*ps = last = p; none = 0;}
        else
            {last->next = p; last = p;}

        if ((p = malloc(STDSIZE)) == NULL){
            puts("not enough heap storage\n");
            fclose(fp);
            return 0;
        }
    }
    if (!none) last->next = NULL;
    free((char *)p);
    fclose(fp);
    if (ferror(fp))
        return 0;
    else
        return 1;
}
```

File reading is terminated upon encountering an end of file or upon encountering an error. Function *ferror* is used to distinguish between these two cases.

Here is the definition of function *writelist* (stored in file *stwrite.c*):

```
#include "student.h"
int writelist(char *db, student *ps)
{
    FILE *fp;

    if ((fp = fopen(db,"w")) == NULL) {
        printf("cannot open file %s\n", db);
        return 0;
    }
    for (; ps != NULL; ps = ps->next)
        if (fwrite((char *) ps,STDSIZE,1,fp)!=1){
            printf("write error on file %s\n",db);
            fclose(fp);
            return 0;
        }
    fclose(fp);
    return 1;
}
```

Function *writelist* writes the records into the file according to the order in which
they appear in the list.

Here is the definition of function *add* (stored in file *stadd.c*):

```c
#include "student.h"
int add(student **ps, student *p)
        /*adds elements while keeping list sorted*/
        /*ps is address of pointer to the head of*/
        /*to which p is to be added*/
{
    student *a, *b;

    if (in(*ps, p->id)) {
        printf("dup. entry for d=%d name=%c %s\n",
                p->id, p->first, p->last);
        printf("entry not added\n");
        return 0;
    }
    if ((a = malloc(STDSIZE)) == NULL){
        puts("not enough heap storage\n");
        return 0;
    }
    a->first = p->first;
    strcpy(a->last, p->last);
    a->id = p->id;
    a->gpa = p->gpa;

    if (*ps == NULL || (*ps)->id > p->id) {
                            /*add at head of list*/
        a->next = *ps;
        *ps = a;
        return 1;
    }
    for(b = *ps; b->next != NULL &&
            (b->next)->id < p->id; b = b->next)
        ; /*find element after which to add p*/
    a->next = b->next; b->next = a;
    return 1;
}
```

A new element *s* is inserted between two elements such that the element before *s* has a smaller *id* than *s* and the element after it has a greater *id*. (The assumption here is that the list elements are kept sorted in increasing order.)

Here is the definition of function *remove* (stored in file *stremove.c*):

```
#include "student.h"
void remove(student **ps, int id)
       /*ps: pointer to the list head*/
       /*id: identifies element to be removed*/
{
     student *last, *cur;

     if (*ps == NULL)
        return;
     if ((*ps)->id == id) {
        free((char *) *ps);
        *ps = (*ps)->next;
        return;
     }
     for (last=*ps, cur=(*ps)->next; cur!=NULL;
          last=cur, cur=cur->next)
        if (cur->id == id) {
           last->next = cur->next;
           free((char *) cur);
           return;
        }
}
```

Finally, here is the definition of function *in* (stored in file *stin.c*):

```
#include "student.h"
student *in(student *ps, int id)
                  /*ps is the list head*/
                  /*id entry is to be removed*/
{
     student *p;

     for (p = ps; p != NULL; p = p->next)
        if (p->id == id)
            return p;
        else if (p->id > id)
            return NULL;
     return NULL;
}
```

To illustrate how these functions are used, we will use them to write a small application: a program to answer student queries about their current grade point average. With this program students can use a specially designated terminal to determine their latest grade point average, much like the way customers at a bank can use a terminal to determine their latest account balance. To make it difficult for students to determine the grade point averages of other students, we will require students to enter both their ids and their last names. The grade point average will be shown only if the entered student id and name match.

Assuming that the student database is stored in file *student.db*, here is the grade point average query program (stored in file *student.c*):

```
#include "student.h"
char db[] = "student.db";
main(void)
{
    student *ps, *s;
            /*ps points to head of student list*/
            /*s is a temporary variable*/
    int id, c; char last[NAMELEN];

    if (readlist("student.db", &ps) == 0)
        puts("error, cannot set up student list");
    for (;;) {
        printf("type id & press enter:");
        if (scanf("%d", &id) == EOF)
            exit(0);
        while((c=getchar()) !='\n');
                            /*skip rest of line*/
        printf("type last name & press enter:");
        if (c == EOF)
            exit(1);
        gets(last);
        if (((s = in(ps, id)) != NULL) &&
                    strcmp(last, s->last) == 0){
            printf("your GPA is %g\n", s->gpa);
            puts("PRESS ENTER TO CLEAR SCREEN\n");
            while((c=getchar()) !='\n');
                            /*skip rest of line*/
            puts("\033[2J");
                    /*clear screen; see [IBM83b]*/
        }
        else
            puts("invalid name & id combination");
    }
}
```

The program will terminate upon encountering an end of file, that is, when a control-Z followed by carriage return is typed on MS-DOS systems (on UNIX systems, an end of file is indicated by typing control-D).

7.3 TREES

Trees are dynamic data structures that are similar to lists. In fact, lists can be considered to be a "degenerate" case of trees. Unlike, a list element, each tree element (node) can have several immediate successors. We shall restrict our discussion to *binary* trees in which an element can have at most two immediate successors: these successors are often called the left and right successors. A tree element that has no successors is called a *leaf*. The pointer that points to the first element of a tree is called the *root* of the tree.

Ordered binary trees are a special class of binary trees which are constructed according to the following ordering rule: the information component (such as the student id) of the left successor of a node *n* precedes (e.g., is less than) the information component of *n*, which in turn precedes the information component of its right successor. Ordered binary trees are used to speed up searches.

To process (access) information stored at all nodes of a tree, the tree elements must be accessed in some order: Here are three commonly used "tree traversal" strategies.

Preorder   Access the left subtree, then the current node, and then the right subtree.

Inorder   Access the current node, then the left subtree, and then the right subtree.

Postorder   Access the right subtree, then the current node, and then the left subtree.

The above tree accessing strategies are defined recursively. Recursion is a very natural tool for processing all the elements of a tree.

To illustrate binary tree manipulation, we will write two functions: *add* to insert a node into an ordered binary tree, and *print* to print, using the preorder processing strategy, the information components of all nodes in the tree.

First, here is the header file (stored in file *tree.h*) that contains the definition of a tree node as well as some function prototypes:

```
#include <stdio.h>
typedef struct node {
    int i;
    struct node *left, *right;
} node;
void add(node **proot, int i);
void print(node *root);
```

Here is function *add* (stored in file *tadd.c*):

```c
#include "tree.h"
#include <stdlib.h>
void add(node **proot, int i)
{
    node *n, *p = *proot;

    if ((n = malloc(sizeof(node))) == NULL){
        puts("not enough heap storage");
        exit(1);
    }
    n->i = i; n->left = NULL; n->right = NULL;

    if (*proot == NULL) {
        *proot = n;
        return;
    }
    for (;;)
        if (n->i < p->i) {
            if (p->left == NULL)
                {p->left = n; return;}
            else
                p = p->left;
        }
        else if (n->i > p->i) {
            if (p->right == NULL)
                {p->right = n; return;}
            else
                p = p->right;
        }
        else
            return;
}
```

Here is function *print* (stored in file *tprint.c*):

```c
#include "tree.h"

void print(node *root)
{
    if (root == NULL)
        return;
    else {
        print(root->left);
        printf("%d\n", root->i);
        print(root->right);
    }
}
```

7.4 PRINTING THE CALL STACK

The ability to access specific locations in memory is essential for systems
programming. Pointers facilitate access to specific memory locations. As an
example, suppose a systems programmer wants to print a portion of the "call
stack" for debugging. When any function is called (including *main*, which is the
first function to be called), the function arguments and the function variables are
allocated in an array on top of the items of the function containing the call. This
array is called a *stack* because the last items allocated on the stack will be the
first ones to be deallocated (the last function call must be completed before the
previous one). In most languages, you cannot examine the call stack dynamically.
But in C you can use pointers to print the data in the call stack.

To print the top portion of the stack, we will write a print function *prntstk* that
takes the address of its first parameter and prints memory locations surrounding
it. By making this function have more than one parameter and calling it with
easily recognizable values, we will be able to quickly identify the values on the
stack.

Here is a program that prints part of the call stack (stored in file *callstk.c*):

```
#include "stdio.h"
#define N 5

/*prnstk: test routine to print part of the */
/*        call stack; N elements below the  */
/*        address where the first parameter */
/*        is placed, and N elements starting*/
/*        with the first parameter address  */
void prntstk(int a, int b, int c)
{
    int d = -8;
    int *p;
    for (p = &a-N; p < &a+N; p++)
        printf("addr=0x%x,val=%d\n",(int) p,*p);
}

main(void)
{
    prntstk(-5, -6, -7);
}
```

The output produced by the above program is shown below:

```
addr=0xa86,val=66
addr=0xa88,val=-8
addr=0xa8a,val=2698
addr=0xa8c,val=2710
addr=0xa8e,val=930
addr=0xa90,val=-5
addr=0xa92,val=-6
addr=0xa94,val=-7
addr=0xa96,val=2720
addr=0xa98,val=1069
```

The negative values assigned to variable d and to the parameters a, b, and c make it very easy to identify their locations on the call stack. Some of the other locations contain information such as hardware register values at the time of the call and the function return address (the address of the code to be executed after returning from the function).

8. EXERCISES

1. What are the pros and cons of using singly-linked lists versus doubly-linked lists?

2. Modify the tree printing algorithm to print the information components of the tree nodes in postorder.

3. What are the problems involved in deleting a tree node? Write a function to delete a binary tree node.

4. Suppose your implementation does not provide the storage allocation function *malloc* and the deallocation function *free*. How will you implement *malloc* and *free*? (Hint: Use a large global static array.) What will you do with the freed storage? Will you keep the freed storage as separate blocks for later reallocation or will you combine it with other free blocks, if possible, to build a larger free block?

CHAPTER 6

C PREPROCESSOR

The C preprocessor, as its name indicates, processes a C program before it is compiled. The preprocessor transforms the program as specified by the preprocessor instructions given in the program. These instructions, which are different from C instructions, begin with the # character. The # character must be the first non-white-space character on a line. Typically, this character is placed in column one. Note that all other instructions in the program should normally be C code (or should lead to C code after preprocessing). However, as far as the C preprocessor is concerned, program text can be arbitrary character sequences.

The C preprocessor is an integral part of the C programming environment. (As mentioned before, there is no counterpart in FORTRAN of the facilities provided by the C preprocessor). Many C facilities are implemented as C preprocessor macros, for example, definitions of constants such as *EOF* and *NULL*, input routines such as *getchar*, the various character processing routines, and the absolute value routine *abs*. Note that the C preprocessor is automatically invoked by the C compiler before a program is compiled.

Specifically, the C preprocessor provides facilities for

- defining and removing macro definitions,

- inserting text from another file by physically including the contents of the specified file, and

- conditional inclusion of text.

C preprocessor facilities are not recognized by the C compiler. Consequently, the program, after having been processed by the C preprocessor, must be valid C code; otherwise, errors will be flagged by the C compiler.

1. MACRO DEFINITIONS

The C preprocessor macro definition facility provides the capability of associating an arbitrary string with an identifier. Every occurrence in the program of an identifier that has been associated with a string is replaced by the associated string. Typically, the macro facility is used for defining symbolic constants, string replacement, and *in-line* functions. The first two items are implemented by using parameterless macros, and the last item by using parameterized macros.

It is important to note that the C preprocessor does not care about the nature of the string associated with an identifier; as far as it is concerned, the string can be arbitrary text. It is the programmer's responsibility to ensure that the string associated with the identifier will result in valid C code after the identifier is replaced by the string, and that it will not lead to a syntax error or a logical error. Syntax errors will be detected by the C compiler, but logical errors resulting from incorrect string definitions or incorrect use of string definitions, like other logical errors, must be discovered and diagnosed by the programmer.

By convention, upper-case letters are used for user-defined macro names (C implementations do not adhere to this convention for pre-defined macros). As mentioned above, the macro definition facility is used to define constants, strings and parameterized macros. Although constant and string definitions are special cases of parameterized macros, they will be discussed separately (to reflect typical use).

1.1 CONSTANT DEFINITIONS

The C preprocessor macro facility is used for defining constants. This is because the C language does not have a constant definition mechanism. ANSI C supports read-only variables but these cannot be used in constant expressions which are required in some situations, e.g., as array bounds.

Constants are defined using macro definitions of the form

```
#define   constant-name   constant-expression
```

Some examples of constant definitions are

```
#define M 64
#define N 16
#define MAX 128
#define SIZE sizeof(int)
#define TOTAL (MAX*SIZE)
#define MASK 077
```

Here are some examples illustrating uses of the above definitions:

```
...
char a[M][N];
int *p;

p = malloc(TOTAL);

for (i=0; i<M; i++) ...

a = a & MASK;
```

Before the above code is compiled, it will be transformed by the C preprocessor to the code shown below by replacing the constant identifiers with their values:

```
    ...
char a[64][16];
int *p;

p = malloc((128*sizeof(int)));

for (i=0; i<64; i++) ...

a = a & 077;
```

Constant definitions make a program more readable and make it easier to modify. For example, suppose that a frequently used constant value is to be changed. If a constant identifier has been used, then this change will require only one modification (to the constant definition). If a constant identifier has not been used, but instead a literal value has been used directly, then every place where the literal has been used will require modification.

If the value of a constant identifier is an expression, then this expression should be enclosed within parentheses to avoid unintended results after the preprocessor has replaced the constant identifier by its value. For example, consider the constant *a* defined as

```
#define M2 M+2
```

Then the expression *M2*3* will be transformed to *M+2*3* and not to *(M+2)*3*. If the latter interpretation is the correct one, as is likely, then *M2* should be defined as

```
#define M2 (M+2)
```

1.2 STRING DEFINITIONS

String definitions, which are similar to constant definitions, are used to give symbolic names to string constants and are also used as abbreviations for C source code. String definitions are of the form

```
#define string-name sequence-of-characters
```

Two example definitions are

```
#define FMT "x=%f, y=%f\n"
#define getchar() getc(stdin)
#define NXT_DATA_LN while(getchar() != '\n')
```

Constant *FMT* defines a string for use with a formatted output function as in the following *printf* function call:

```
printf(FMT, x, y);
```

The preprocessor transforms the macro call

```
getchar()
```

to the code

```
getc(stdin)
```

A semicolon was not given at the end of *getc*(*stdin*) in the definition of *getchar* because *getchar* can then look and be used like an ordinary function call. Here are two examples:

```
c = getchar();
while ((c == getchar()) != EOF) ...
```

The code associated with *NXT_DATA_LN* skips to the beginning of the next input line. Each use of

```
NXT_DATA_LN;
```

is replaced by the code

```
while(getchar() != '\n');
```

1.3 MACROS (IN-LINE FUNCTIONS)

Macros are essentially in-line functions. In the case of ordinary functions, a function call is translated into a jump to the code for the function body and at the end of the function a return jump to the statement following the function call is generated by the compiler. In case of macros, a macro call is textually replaced by the macro body after appropriately replacing the parameters with the corresponding arguments. Because of the textual replacement performed by the C preprocessor, no jumps to the beginning of the macro body and back from the end of the macro body are necessary.

Macros can lead to faster code than functions and should be used

- especially when implementing very small routines that are called from many places in the program, or

- when implementing a routine which is called from a small number of places in the program but which is called frequently during program execution.

The use of macros speeds up program execution due to the absence of jumps and due to the absence of the run-time copying of argument values to parameters. In case of very small macros or macros that are called only from a few places in the program, the size of the object file may also decrease. In other cases, the program size may actually increase.

Besides textual replacement of the macro calls by the corresponding macro bodies, there are other important differences between macros and functions. For example, macro names, unlike function names, cannot be passed as function arguments and side effects in macro arguments can lead to unexpected results (this is discussed later).

In a parameterized macro definition, the parameter names are specified along with the macro name and the macro body:

#define *macro-name* $(p_1, p_2, ..., p_n)$ *macro-body*

p_i are the macro parameters.

A macro call has the form

macro-name $(a_1, a_2, ..., a_n)$

where a_i are the macro arguments. This macro call will be replaced by the corresponding macro body, but only after each occurrence of the parameter p_i in the macro body has been replaced by the corresponding argument a_i.

Let us now look at some examples of parameterized macros. Here are some examples taken from the standard C header files such as *stdio.h* and *ctype.h*:

```
#define  putchar(c)  putc(c,stdout)
#define  rewind(fp)  fseek(fp,0L,0)

#define  toupper(c)  (islower(c)?((c)-('a'-'A')):(c))
#define  tolower(c)  (isupper(c)?((c)+('a'-'A')):(c))

#define  abs(a)  ((a)<0 ? -(a):(a))
#define  max(a,b)  ((a)>(b)?(a):(b))
#define  min(a,b)  ((a)<(b)?(a):(b))
```

One interesting question to ask is why are there so many parentheses in the definitions of the macros *toupper*, *tolower*, *abs*, *max*, and *min*. The answer is safety and that is the focus of the next section.

To illustrate preprocessor expansion of parameterized macro calls, consider the call

```
max(x,y)
```

This call will be replaced by the expression

```
((x)>(y)?(x):(y))
```

Similarly the nested calls

```
max(x,max(y,z))
```

will be replaced by the expression

```
((x)>(((y)>(z)?(y):(z)))?(x):(((y)>(z)?(y):(z))))
```

Here are some examples of user-defined macro definitions:

```
#define SQR(x)  ((x)*(x))
#define PRINTI(x)  printf("x = %d\n", x)
```

PRINTI simplifies the printing of an integer variable's name along with its value. For example, the name of an integer variable *a* and its value can be printed as

```
PRINTI(a);
```

This call is replaced in the C source code by the body of *PRINTI* but after parameter *x* has been replaced by the argument *a*:

```
printf("a = %d\n", a);
```

A macro cannot be called from within its own body. In other words, the preprocessor macro facility does not support recursion.

1.4 SAFETY & GOOD PROGRAMMING PRACTICE

As in the case of functions, arbitrary expressions (arbitrary character sequences as far as the C preprocessor is concerned) can be given as arguments in a macro call. In the case of a function, the expression is evaluated and the result is the value assigned to the corresponding parameter. However, in the case of macros, each parameter is textually replaced at compile time by the corresponding unevaluated argument. Consequently, programmers should be careful when calling macros with arbitrary expressions. For example, parameter references in the macro body should be enclosed in parentheses.

As an illustration of the hazards that can be encountered if macro parameters are not enclosed in parentheses, consider the definition of the macro *SQR* which was given earlier:

```
#define SQR(x)  ((x)*(x))
```

At a first glance, it appears that each of the three pairs of parentheses is superfluous. As it turns out, each pair of parentheses is essential. Suppose, for example, that we had not used these parentheses and we had instead defined *SQR* as

```
#define SQR(x)  x*x
```

As long as *SQR* is called with simple variables and with adjacent operators having a lower precedence than * there is no problem. The C preprocessor replaces the call

```
SQR(a)
```

by the text

```
a*a
```

which is what we want. Problems arise when *SQR* is called with arguments that are expressions. For example, the call

```
SQR(a+1)
```

will be expanded by the preprocessor into the expression

```
a+1*a+1
```

which is equivalent to the expression $2a+1$ and not to the expected expression $(a+1)*(a+1)$. This problem can be avoided by enclosing each occurrence of every macro parameter in the macro body within parentheses. If we do this, then the revised definition of *SQR* will look like

```
#define SQR(x)  (x)*(x)
```

Now the call $SQR(a+1)$ will be expanded to

```
(a+1)*(a+1)
```

which is what we want.

Enclosing each parameter within parentheses does not remove all potential problem situations. Consider the following expression

```
b/SQR(a)
```

in which we want to divide *b* by the square of *a*. Unfortunately, *SQR* will not work correctly and the value of the above expression will be just *b*. This is because the C preprocessor will expand the above call to

```
b/a*a
```

which is equivalent to the expression

```
(b/a)*a
```

This problem can be avoided by putting the whole macro body within parentheses, which leads us to the original definition of *SQR*:

```
#define SQR(x)  ((x)*(x))
```

Finally, there is one more problem that can lead to errors when using macros: macro arguments with side effects. An expression with side effects is one that, when evaluated, causes a change in the value of a variable. Examples of expressions with side effects are expressions containing the assignment, the increment and the decrement operators. Giving an expression with side effects as a macro argument can cause problems if the corresponding parameter occurs more than once in the macro body. Each instance of the parameter in the macro body is replaced by the unevaluated expression argument. Consequently, each time the expression is evaluated, side effects will occur, once for each occurrence of the parameter in the macro body.

As an example, consider the macro call

```
SQR(a++)
```

which we expect to return a^2 and to increment a by 1. Unfortunately, this will not happen because the above call will be replaced by the expression

```
((a++)*(a++))
```

which, depending upon the compiler, will either evaluate to a^2 or a^2+1. In both cases, a will be incremented *twice* by 1.

Therefore, it is good programming practice to

- enclose all instances of a macro parameter in the macro body within parentheses,
- enclose the macro body in parentheses, and
- avoid calling macros with expressions that have side effects.

1.5 REMOVING (ERASING) MACRO DEFINITIONS

Macros definitions must be removed explicitly before the same macro name is defined as a new macro. Macro definitions are removed using the *#undef* instruction which has the form

```
#undef name
```

Note that conditional compilation instructions (to be discussed later) can be used to determine whether or not a macro has been defined and then generate code based on this information.

2. SETS: AN EXAMPLE OF PARAMETERIZED MACROS

A set is a collection of objects no two of which are alike. Set operations include adding an element to and deleting an element from a set, checking set membership, taking the union, intersection and difference of two sets, iterating through all the elements of a set, determining the size of a set, and so forth.

One strategy for implementing a set is to use one word of memory for recording the elements present in the set. Each element of the set is assigned one of the bits: a zero bit value (bit off) indicates that the element is not in the set while a one bit value (bit on) indicates presence of the element in the set. This implementation is very simple and straightforward, but it does have one limitation: the maximum set size is limited to the number of bits in the word.

We will now define operations for manipulating a set of integers (from 0 to *MAXSETSIZE*-1); these operations will be defined as macros because they are very small, and the overhead of using functions will be significantly more than the cost of the actual set operations. Also, it will not be straightforward to define a function equivalent of the *foreach* loop for iterating through each element of the set.

Here is the header file for defining and manipulating set variables (stored in file *set.h*):

```
#define SET unsigned long
#define MAXSETSIZE (sizeof(SET)*8)

#define in(i, s) ((s) & (((SET) 1) << (i)))
#define add(i, s) ((s) | (((SET) 1) << (i)))
#define remove(i, s) ((s) & ~(((SET) 1) << (i)))
#define union(s, t) ((s) | (t))
#define intersection(s, t) ((s) & (t))
#define difference(s, t) ((s) & ~(t))
#define foreach(j, s) for(j=0;j<MAXSETSIZE;j++)
```

A set is represented using the largest unsigned integer allowed, that is, by using an *unsigned long* value. In general, only unsigned integers should be used for bit manipulation because right shifting an unsigned word causes zero to be filled in the leftmost bit, while right shifting a signed word causes the sign bit to be propagated.

Checking to see whether or not an element is present in a set (operation *in*) is done by constructing a word with just the bit corresponding to the element having the value one and then performing a *bitwise and* with the set. If the element in question is present in the set, then the result of the *bitwise and* will be non-zero; otherwise, it will be zero. Element addition (operation *add*) is similar to set membership checking except that a *bitwise or* operation is performed instead of the *bitwise and*. Implementations of the other operations, i.e., *remove, union, intersection*, and *difference* are similarly straightforward and are therefore not explained here.

The *foreach* loop is a customized loop for iterating over all the elements of a set. It is not possible to write such a customized loop without macros (of course, one can always write the code in the definition of *foreach* directly in the program text). Notice the use of the backslash to continue the definition of *foreach* on to a new line.

Here are some examples illustrating use of the above macros:

```
SET s = 0, t = 0, z;
int i;

s = add(1,s);
s = add(2,s);
s = add(30,s); /*MAXSETSIZE == 32*/
s = remove(2, s);
z=intersection(s,t);

foreach(i, z) printf("%d ", i);
```

3. FILE INCLUSION

Typically, C program declarations that are used in several source files are kept in headers file. The contents of the header files are then physically included in the files needing the declarations by using the C preprocessor *#include* instruction. FORTRAN does not have a file inclusion capability, although some FORTRAN compilers may provide such a facility. The *#include* instruction has two forms:

```
#include "fname"
#include <fname>
```

fname is the name of the file to be included (*fname* can also contain path information). The *#include* instruction can be nested, i.e., the included file can itself contain *#include* instructions. The maximum level of nesting is implementation dependent.

The only difference between the two forms of the *#include* instruction is that the first form (with the file name in quotes) looks for the specified file in the current directory before searching other implementation- or user-specified directories. (As a compile-time option, most C compilers allow the user to specify additional directories that are to be searched for the file to be included.) The second form of the *#include* instruction (with the file name in angle brackets) does not look for the file in the current directory.

The first form of the *#include* instruction (with the file name in quotes) is normally used for including user header files and the second form (with the file name in angle brackets) is used for including standard library header files.

A path name, that is, a file name with directory information, can be given instead of a simple file name. On the MS-DOS system, backslashes are used to separate components of the path name while on UNIX systems slashes are used. Many MS-DOS system C compilers will accept both slashes and backslashes in the path name. For example, you can specify the path name as

```
/simulation/debug.h
```

or as

```
\simulation\debug.h
```

Although the *#include* instruction is typically used to include header files, any file, including C source files, can be included with it.

4. CONDITIONAL COMPILATION

Conditional compilation can be used to specify default macro definitions, to generate different versions of the same program and to avoid multiple file inclusions. The C preprocessor allows conditional compilation to be based on the value of a constant expression and whether or not a symbol has been defined.

4.1 CONDITIONAL COMPILATION BASED ON THE VALUE OF CONSTANT EXPRESSIONS

The *#if* instruction is used for conditionally compiling C code based on the value of a constant expression. This instruction has the forms

```
#if constant-expression
     true-alternative-text
#endif
```

```
#if constant-expression
     true-alternative-text
#else
     false-alternative-text
#endif
```

Like C, the preprocessor treats a non-zero value as true and a zero as false. The text in each alternative can be arbitrary sequence of characters including preprocessor instructions. Remember that the preprocessor does not understand C. It only understands lines beginning with the character #; to the C preprocessor, every thing else is just a sequence of characters.

The preprocessor operator *defined* can be used to determine whether or not an identifier has been previously defined using the *#define* instruction. This operator, as mentioned earlier, can be used in constant expressions.

4.2 CONDITIONAL COMPILATION BASED ON SYMBOL DEFINITION

The *#ifdef* and *#ifndef* instructions are used to conditionally compile code depending upon whether or not the specified symbol has been defined. (The specific string associated with the symbol is not significant.) The *#ifdef* instruction has the forms

```
#ifdef symbol
      true-alternative-text
#endif

#ifdef symbol
      true-alternative-text
#else
      false-alternative-text
#endif
```

The #ifndef instruction is similar to the #ifdef instruction, but it does the reverse. Instead of checking to see if a symbol has been defined, it checks to see if the symbol has *not* been defined. The #ifdef and #ifndef instructions can be used to provide default constant (or default macro) definitions. For example, if an array size has not been explicitly specified, then a default size can be used:

```
#ifndef MAX_SIZE
#define MAX_SIZE 128
#endif
```

If identifier *MAX_SIZE* has defined before the above instructions are encountered, then it will not be given a new value; otherwise, it will be defined to have the value 128.

As another example of conditional compilation, suppose you are writing a C program that contains machine-dependent code for the IBM PC, Apple^{TM}, and Rainbow^{TM} computers. When compiling code for a specific computer, only code for this particular computer is to be compiled. Here is how code that is to be conditionally compiled can be written:

```
#ifdef IBMPC
      code for the IBM PC computer
#endif
#ifdef APPLE
      code for the Apple computer
#endif
#ifdef RAINBOW
      code for the Rainbow computer
#endif
```

Now suppose you want to compile the program for the IBM PC. Then you must in an appropriate header file, which is to be included by all functions containing machine-dependent code, define the symbol *IBMPC*:

```
#define IBMPC 1
```

When compiling code for the Apple or the Rainbow computers, just replace this definition by a definition of the identifiers *APPLE* or *RAINBOW*, as appropriate.

Note that the *defined* operator can be used with the *#if* statement to match the functionality of the *#ifdef* and the *#ifndef* statements. This operator has been introduced in ANSI C and was not present in K&R C.

4.3 PREDEFINED IDENTIFIERS FOR CONDITIONAL COMPILATION

Many C compilers predefine some identifiers for the convenience of the programmer to facilitate conditional compilation. Typically, the pre-defined symbols specify the computer and the operating system on which the program is being compiled. For instance, on VAX computers, many C compilers will automatically define the symbol *vax*.

5. AVOIDING MULTIPLE FILE INCLUSIONS

Conditional compilation can also be invaluable when writing large programs consisting of many files that are written by several programmers. As an example, consider a function *test.c* that includes two header files, *sim.h* and *list.h*, as follows:

```
#include "sim.h"
#include "list.h"
```

Now suppose that the header file *sim.h* is modified to include the header file *list.h* because the declarations in *sim.h* have been changed and they now require the declarations in *list.h*. The two *#include* instructions shown above will cause *list.h* to be included twice in *test.c* leading to errors and warning messages which will be generated when *test.c* is compiled. The double inclusion of *list.h* can be avoided by using conditional compilation in conjunction with the following convention:

1. An identifier is associated with each header file to indicate whether or not the header file has been included.

2. Before including a file, check to determine whether or not the associated identifier is defined. If yes, then the file has already been included, and it should not be included again. Otherwise, include the file and define its associated identifier.

Continuing our example, suppose that identifiers *SIM* and *LIST* are associated with the header files *sim.h* and *list.h*. File *sim.h* includes file *list.h* as follows:

```
#ifndef LIST
#define LIST 1
#include "list.h"
#endif
```

Now the above paradigm will be used to include both the files *list.h* and *sim.h* in *test.c*:

```
#ifndef SIM
#define SIM 1
#include "sim.h"
#endif

#ifndef LIST
#define LIST 1
#include "list.h"
#endif
```

Use of the above paradigm ensures that file *list.h* will not be included twice in *test.c*.

6. EXERCISES

1. Write a macro *INT* to simulate the FORTRAN function *INT* that takes a single or double precision real value x and returns the largest integer less than or equal to x.

2. Define *CLS* as an instruction to clear the screen (like the MS-DOS CLS instruction). It is to be used as

    ```
    CLS;
    ```

3. List the pros and cons of using functions versus using macros.

4. Write a function version of the macro *PRINTI* (see Section 1.3) and then compare the macro and function versions.

5. What are the pros and cons of using enumeration types instead of the symbolic preprocessor constant definitions and vice versa?

6. How will you implement sets of size greater than the number of bits in an *unsigned long* type? Sketch the implementation of the set operations.

CHAPTER 7

LARGE EXAMPLES

Three relatively large examples are given in this chapter to give the reader a better idea of how real programs are written using C. These programs illustrate a variety of C facilities and programming techniques such as

- passing two-dimensional arrays as arguments,
- program modularization,
- using external variables for inter-function communication,
- structures,
- reducing program size and enhancing readability with the preprocessor,
- type conversions,
- reading blocks of data from files and writing them to files,
- random file access,
- function *static* variables,
- using escape sequences to control the hardware, i.e., clear the screen and turn reverse video on/off, and
- a rare use of the *goto* statement.

The first example is illustrates the use of C for scientific programming, the primary application domain for FORTRAN. The other two examples illustrate application domains for which FORTRAN is typically not used: the second example is a simplified version of a banking application and the third example is a simple document formatting program.

1. TEMPERATURE DISTRIBUTION

The problem is to write a program to compute the temperature distribution over a thin rectangular plate. The boundaries of the plate are maintained at a constant temperature *boundary_temp* which is supplied as input. The temperature distribution is computed by representing the plate as a 2-dimensional array *plate_temp* with $M \times N$ elements. Each element corresponds to a point on an $M \times N$ grid mapped on to the plate. The algorithm used to compute the "steady-state" temperature distribution is as follows:

1. The boundary elements of *plate_temp* are initialized to *boundary_temp* and its internal elements are initialized to *boundary_temp*/2.
2. A new temperature is computed for each element by taking the average of the four surrounding elements.
3. Step 2 is repeated until the value of every element changes less than the stopping limit *stop_limit* which is a small value. *stop_limit* is supplied as input.

Increasing the number of elements of the array *plate_temp* will yield a more detailed temperature distribution but it will also increase the time required to compute the distribution.

The program to compute the temperature distribution is structured as follows: the *main* program reads the values for *boundary_temp* and *stop_limit*. It then initializes the plate array *plate_temp*, prints it (the initial temperature distribution), calls function *plate_temp_distr* to compute the temperature distribution, and thens print the final temperature distribution.

Here are the declarations that will be used in the program (stored in file *plate.h*):

```
#define M 10
#define N 10
void plate_temp_distr(float t[M][N],int m,int n,float eps);
```

The interesting thing to note is the declaration of the first parameter, i.e., *t*, in the prototype of function *plate_temp_distr*. *t* is a 2-dimensional array parameters whose bounds have been explicitly specified. The first dimension of an array parameter can be omitted but all other dimensions must be explicitly specified. Thus the alternative function prototype

```
void plate_temp_distr(float t[][N], int m, int n, float eps);
```

is legal but the function prototype

```
void plate_temp_distr(float t[][], int m, int n, float eps);
```

would be illegal.

The type of *t* is a pointer to an array of *N float* elements. Hence the prototype of *plate_temp_distr* can also be written as

```
void plate_temp_distr(float (*t)[N], int m, int n, float eps);
```

The parentheses are required because operator [] has a higher precedence than *.

Here is the main program (stored in file *plate.c*):

```
#include <stdio.h>
#include "plate.h"
main(void)
{
    float plate_temp[M][N];
    int i, j;
    float boundary_temp, stop_limit;

    scanf("%f", &boundary_temp);
    scanf("%f", &stop_limit);

    /*initialize plate temperatures*/
        for (i=0; i < N; i++)
            for (j=0; j < N; j++)
                if (i==0 || i==M-1 || j==0 || j==N-1)
                    plate_temp[i][j] = boundary_temp;
                else
                    plate_temp[i][j] = boundary_temp/2.0;

    /*print initial plate temp. and stopping limit*/
        for (i=0; i < N; i++) {
            for (j=0; j < N; j++)
                printf("%g ", plate_temp[i][j]);
            putchar('\n');
        }
        printf("stop limit = %g\n\n", stop_limit);

    plate_temp_distr(plate_temp, M, N, stop_limit);

    /*print final plate temperatures*/
        for (i=0; i < N; i++) {
            for (j=0; j < N; j++)
                printf("%g ", plate_temp[i][j]);
            putchar('\n');
        }
}
```

C does not have the implied-*DO* loop of FORTRAN nor does it provide facilities to print all the array elements by just specifying the array to be printed. Array elements must be printed with explicit loops.

Finally, here is function *plate_temp_distr* that computes the temperature distribution (stored in file *tdistr.c*):

```
#include "plate.h"
#define ABS(x) ((x) ? (x) : -(x))
void plate_temp_distr(float t[M][N],int m,int n,float eps)
{
    int i = m, j = n;
    int done;
    float old;

    do {
        done = 1;
        for (i=1; i < m - 1; i++)
            for (j=1; j < n - 1; j++) {
                old = t[i][j];
                t[i][j] = (t[i-1][j]+t[i+1][j]+
                                  t[i][j-1]+t[i][j+1])/4.0;
                done = done && (ABS(t[i][j]-old) <= eps);
            }
    } while (!done);
}
```

2. THE BANK TELLER PROGRAM

The problem is to write a program which will be used by a bank teller when interacting with a customer to update and query the bank database. For simplicity, we will assume that the bank is a very small one and that there is only one teller. This assumption ensures that only one program interacts with the database at any given time which frees us from worrying about problems that arise when multiple programs simultaneously query and update the same database records.

The bank teller can interact with the database in several ways. Teller interactions with the database are called *bank transactions*. A bank transaction can have one of the following forms:

t
t a_1
t a_1 a_2
t a_1 a_2 a_3

where *t* is a code specifying a bank transaction and a_1, a_2, and a_3 are transaction arguments. The description of the bank teller transactions along with their codes is given below. As appropriate, each transaction prints the requested information or it prints information about the bank account in question to show that the transaction was carried out successfully:

    open new account (code "o")   Takes a client name as its argument, opens a new account, and returns the new account number.

    close account (code "c")   Takes an account number as its argument and closes the specified account.

deposit money (code "d")	Takes two arguments–the account number and the amount to be deposited. It increments the balance in the specified account by the specified deposit.
withdraw money (code "w")	Takes two arguments–the account number and the amount to be withdrawn. A withdrawal is allowed only if there are sufficient funds in the specified account. If a withdrawal is allowed, then the account balance is reduced by the specified withdrawal amount.
transfer money (code "t")	Takes three arguments–the account numbers for the withdrawal and the deposit, and the amount to be transferred. Transfer of funds between the accounts is allowed only if the source account has sufficient funds.
balance (code "b")	Takes an account number as an argument and prints the balance in the account.
help (code "h")	Prints transaction codes and their arguments.
print (code "p")	Prints information about all accounts (appropriate only for extremely small banks).
quit (code "q")	Terminates the bank teller program.

The bank database is kept in a file named *bank.db* with the data being stored in the following format:

total number of accounts (including closed ones)
account$_1$
account$_2$
...
account$_n$

Each account has three fields: account number, customer name, and balance. Closed accounts will be indicated by a zero account number. One question to ask is why not physically remove the information about a closed account from the file. One important reason for not doing this is that banks like to keep information about closed accounts for any questions that may need to be answered at a later time. In practice, information about closed accounts is physically removed from bank databases after a specified time period. Another reason for not physically removing information is that physically deleting an account requires more work than just changing the account number to zero; specifically, all the accounts after the closed account must be shifted to close up the gap that arises because of the closed account.

The bank teller program that will be shown here is partitioned into several modules: the header file, the file containing the main program, and the files containing the functions implementing the bank transactions. Let us first look at the header file, *bnk.h*, which is included by all the other modules because it contains declarations needed by them:

```
#include <stdio.h>

#define  LL 64
#define  INTI (int) sizeof(int)
#define  INTL (long) sizeof(int)
#define  ACTI (int) sizeof(account)
#define  ACTL (long) sizeof(account)
#define  SUCCESS 1
#define  FAILURE 0

#define  NXT_DATA_LN while(getchar() != '0)

typedef struct {
    int no;    /* == 0 means closed */
    char name[LL];
    double bal;
} account;

extern FILE *fp;
extern int n;

int balance(int no);
int closeact(int no);
int deposit(int no, double amt);
void help(void);
void openact(char name[]);
void printact(account *a);
void printdb(void);
int withdraw(int no, double amt);
```

The interesting aspect of this header file is the use of the C preprocessor to define abbreviations representing C source code. For instance, the random file access functions, such as *fseek*, *fread* and *fwrite*, require that the record size argument should be of either the type *int* or the type *long* depending upon the function. However, the *sizeof* operator, which is used to compute the record size, returns *unsigned* values. Consequently, the cast operator must be used to convert the value returned by *sizeof* operator to the type required by the file access functions. Without the use of the preprocessor constant definitions—*INTI*, *INTL*, *ACTI*, and *ACTL*—calls to the file functions (which we shall see later) will be textually long and this may make the code hard to read in some cases.

Another example of code abbreviation is the symbol *NXT_DATA_LN* which is defined as a loop that skips to the beginning of the next line. Note the absence of the semicolon at the end of the loop. This means that every use of

NXT_DATA_LN must be followed by a semicolon that will make each use of *NXT_DATA_LN* look like a C statement.

Structure type *account* specifies components for holding information associated with a single bank account. This makes it convenient to manipulate account information. For example, a single *account* variable can be used to store all the information associated with one account and giving this variable as an argument to a function provides the function with all the information about the account.

External variables *fp* and *n* are used for inter-function communication. Although parameters could also have been used, it is more convenient to use external variables for inter-function communication because the same variables are to be passed as arguments every time. This makes the function calls shorter and increases program efficiency (in this case by a small amount) by eliminating the need to copy the argument values to the corresponding parameters.

The two external variables, *fp*, and *n*, are used by most of the functions in the bank teller program. *fp* and *n* will be defined only in function *main* but their declarations will be included in all files that refer to them. Variable *fp* is initialized to the bank database file *bank.db*, and *n* is initialized to the total number of accounts (including closed ones). Because *main* contains the definitions of these variables, it is not necessary to include their declarations in *main* (provided they are used after their definitions are encountered). Nevertheless, their declarations are included in *main* as a side effect of including file *bnk.h* which, among other things, contains their declarations. Note that file *bnk.h* is included in *main* for the declarations of other variables that are needed by *main*. Redundant declarations are harmless provided they do not clash with each other or with the corresponding definitions.

The *main* program (stored in file *bnk.c*) consists essentially of one big *switch* statement. It reads the transaction code and the transaction arguments entered by the bank teller and then calls the appropriate function. Both external variables *fp* and *n* are defined and initialized in function *main*:

```
#include "bnk.h"

FILE *fp;
int n = 0;   /*number of accounts including*/
             /*deleted ones*/

main(void)
{
    char name[LL];
    int code, no, no2;
    double amt;

    puts("Good Morning!");
    if ((fp = fopen("bank.db", "r+"))==NULL) {
        puts("error, cannot open \"bank.db\"");
        exit(1);
    }
    fread((char *) &n, INTI, 1, fp);
    for (;;) {
        switch (code = getchar()) {
        case 'o':
            openact(gets(name));
            break;
        case 'c':
        case 'b':
            scanf("%d", &no);
            NXT_DATA_LN;
            if (code == 'c')
                closeact(no);
            else
                balance(no);
            break;
        case 'd':
        case 'w':
            scanf("%d%lf", &no, &amt);
            NXT_DATA_LN;
            if (code == 'd')
                deposit(no, amt);
            else
                withdraw(no, amt);
            break;
        case 't':
            scanf("%d%d%lf", &no, &no2, &amt);
            NXT_DATA_LN;
            if (withdraw(no, amt) == SUCCESS)
                deposit(no2, amt);
            break;
        case 'h':
            NXT_DATA_LN;
            help();
            break;
        case 'p':
            NXT_DATA_LN;
```

```
            printdb();
            break;
        case 'q':
            fclose(fp);
            exit(0);
        default:
            NXT_DATA_LN;
            puts("error, try again");
        }
    }
}
```

Function *main* opens the database file and eventually closes it when the bank teller quits by typing the transaction code "q". Other functions do not have to worry about opening and closing the database file.

Money transfer from one account to another is treated as a two-stage transaction: a successful withdrawal followed by a deposit. This allows functions used for withdrawing and depositing money to be used also for inter-account money transfer. This eliminates the need for writing a new function just for doing inter-account money transfer. Note that writing programs as a collection of small and appropriately parameterized functions encourages the reuse of existing software.

Notice the use of the backslash to include the double quote character in a string literal given as the argument in the *puts* function call:

```
puts("error, cannot open \"bank.db\"");
```

As mentioned earlier, preceding a character by a backslash either suppresses the special role of the character in the language (as in "\"") or gives the character some special meaning (as in "\n" which denotes the new-line character).

Opening an account is a matter of rewinding the file (moving to the beginning of the file), writing the total number of accounts (one more than before), seeking (moving) to the end of the file, and writing a record for the new account. Here is function *openact* (stored in file *bnkopn.c*), which is used to open a new account:

```c
#include "bnk.h"

void openact(char name[])
{
    account a;

    a.no = ++n;
    strcpy(a.name, name);
    a.bal = 0;

    rewind(fp);
    fwrite((char *) &n, INTI, 1, fp);
    fseek(fp, (long) (INTL+(n-1)*ACTL), 0);
            /*move to end of file*/
    fwrite((char *) &a, ACTI, 1, fp);
    printact(&a);
}
```

As mentioned earlier, an account is closed by simply setting the account number to 0. Here is the function *closeact* (stored in file *bnkclo.c*):

```c
#include "bnk.h"

int closeact(int no)
{
    account a;

    if (no > n) {
        printf("error, act %d non existent\n",no);
        return FAILURE;
    }
    rewind(fp);
    fseek(fp, INTL+(no-1)*ACTL, 1);
    fread((char *) &a, ACTI, 1, fp);
    if (a.no == no) {
        printact(&a);
        if (a.bal == 0.0)
            printf("account closed\n");
        else {
            printf("acct. closed, pay $%.2f\n", a.bal);
            a.bal = 0.0;
        }
        a.no = 0;
        fseek(fp, -ACTL, 1);
        fwrite((char *) &a, ACTI, 1, fp);
        return SUCCESS;
    }
    printf("error, act %d already closed\n", no);
    return FAILURE;
}
```

Function *deposit* is called when a client makes a deposit (stored in file *bnkdep.c*):

```
#include "bnk.h"

int deposit(int no, double amt)
{
    account a;

    if (no > n) {
        printf("error, act %d non existent\n",no);
        return FAILURE;
    }
    if (amt < 0) {
        puts("error, deposit should be positive");
        return FAILURE;
    }
    rewind(fp);
    fseek(fp, INTL+(no-1)*ACTL, 1);
    fread((char *) &a, ACTI, 1, fp);
    if (a.no == no) {
        a.bal += amt;   /*note, no overflow check*/
        fseek(fp, -ACTL, 1);
        fwrite((char *) &a, ACTI, 1, fp);
        printact(&a);
        return SUCCESS;
    }
    printf("error, account %d is closed\n", no);
    return FAILURE;
}
```

Function *withdraw* (stored in file *bnkwit.c*) is called when a client wants to withdraw money:

```
#include "bnk.h"

int withdraw(int no, double amt)
{
    account a;

    if (no > n) {
        printf("error, act %d non existent\n",no);
        return FAILURE;
    }
    if (amt < 0) {
        puts("error, withdrawl should be positive");
        return FAILURE;
    }
    rewind(fp);
    fseek(fp, INTL+(no-1)*ACTL, 1);
    fread((char *) &a, ACTI, 1, fp);
    if (a.no == no) {
        if (a.bal - amt < 0) {
            puts("insuffient funds in account");
            printact(&a);
            return FAILURE;
        }
        a.bal -= amt;
        fseek(fp, -ACTL, 1);
        fwrite((char *) &a, ACTI, 1, fp);
        printact(&a);
        return SUCCESS;
    }
    printf("error, act %d is closed\n", no);
    return FAILURE;
}
```

Function *balance* (stored in file *bnkbal.c*) is used to print the account balance:

```
#include "bnk.h"

int balance(int no)
{
    account a;

    if (no > n) {
        printf("error, act %d non existent\n", no);
        return FAILURE;
    }
    rewind(fp);
    fseek(fp, INTL+(no-1)*ACTL, 1);
    fread((char *) &a, ACTI, 1, fp);
    if (a.no == no) {
        printact(&a); return SUCCESS;
    }
    printf("error, account %d is closed\n", no);
    return FAILURE;
}
```

Here is the *help* function (stored in file *bnkhlp.c*) which prints information about transaction codes and their arguments for the convenience of the bank teller:

```
#include "bnk.h"

void help(void)
{
    puts("\033[2J"); /*clear screen*/
    puts("\033[7mo\033[0mpen Firstname Lastname");
            /*\033[7m turns on reverse video */
            /*\033[0m turns off reverse video*/
    puts("\033[7mc\033[0mlose ActNo");
    puts("\033[7md\033[0meposit ActNo Amount");
    puts("\033[7mw\033[0mithdraw ActNo Amount");
    puts("\033[7mt\033[0mransfer From To Amount");
    puts("\033[7mb\033[0malance ActNo");
    puts("\033[7mh\033[0melp");
    puts("\033[7mq\033[0muit");
    puts("");
}
```

Note the use of escape sequences to clear the screen ("\033[2J") and to turn reverse video on ("\033[7m") and off ("\033[0m"). Escape sequences are not printed. Instead they just change the monitor display characteristics. If you are interested in more details about escape sequences, see the *IBM DOS Technical Reference Manual* [IBM83b] or a technical reference manual appropriate for your hardware.

The next two functions (stored in file *bnkprt.c*) are straightforward: *printact* prints an account record and *printdb* prints the whole database:

```
#include "bnk.h"

void printact(account *a)
{
    printf("act no=%d name=%s balance=%.2f\n",
                    a->no, a->name, a->bal);
}

void printdb(void)
{
    int i;
    account a;

    rewind(fp);
    puts("\033[2J"); /*clear screen*/
    printf("Number of Accounts=%d\n", n);
    fseek(fp, INTL, 1);
    for (i=0; i<n; i++) {
        fread((char *) &a, ACTI, 1, fp);
        printact(&a);
    }
}
```

To produce an executable form of the bank teller program, the component modules must be compiled and linked together.

3. THE TEXT FORMATTER

The problem is to write a simple "batch-oriented" text formatter (in contrast to a "wysiwyg" formatter)* that takes a text document, interspersed with text formatting commands, and formats the document text as specified by the formatting commands. These commands begin with the character "@" in column one.

By default, the formatter operates in the *fill* and *justify* modes in which as many words as possible are fitted on a line. In the justify mode blanks are inserted between words, whenever necessary, to right justify the text. Note that blanks are not inserted before the first word or after the last word; otherwise, the text will not be left and right justified, respectively. Blanks are also not inserted before a punctuation mark, such as a comma, that immediately follows a word without a

---

* When using a batch-oriented formatter, the formatting commands are interspersed with the document text. The formatted version of the document can be viewed only after the document is processed with the formatter. It is only then that you get to see the effects of the formatting commands. In contrast, with a "wysiwyg" (what-you-see-is-what-you-get) formatter, you see the formatted output as it is entered into the computer. The wysiwyg formatter interprets the formatting commands right away; it does not wait until after you have entered the whole document.

separating blank.

The fill mode can be turned off. In case of the no-fill or copy mode all input lines, except formatting commands, are copied from the input to the output without any formatting, until a formatting command specifying a change to the fill mode is encountered.

Here are the formatting commands that are to be implemented:

@p Begin a new paragraph.

@np Begin a new page.

@nf Turn off fill mode, that is, switch to fill mode.

@fi Restore fill mode.

The formatter program is partitioned into several modules each of which contains one function. These functions are listed below:

main Decision making function that gets tokens, assembles, and prints lines.

justify Function that justifies a line by filling blanks.

token Function that returns the token type as the function result and the token itself in the function argument; tokens are items such as a space, a word or a format specifier.

printline Print line function.

error Function for printing an error message.

For this simple formatter, it was convenient to think of a word as a sequence of text characters (excluding those making up the formatting commands) terminated by a blank, a new line, or a formatting command. Consequently, punctuation marks immediately following a word are considered to be part of the word itself ensuring that they will not be separated from the word by being put on the next line or by blanks inserted in the line to right justify it.

Here is the file *fmt.h* which contains declarations used by the various modules:

```
#include <stdio.h>

        /*token type*/
#define SPACE     0
#define NOFILL    1
#define FILL      2
#define NEWPAGE   3
#define NL        4
#define PARA      5
#define WORD      6

#define LL 80
#define WL 80

extern char word[][WL];
    /*word[i] contains word i of current line*/
    /*only first dimension can be unspecified*/
extern int spaces[];
    /*spaces[i]: word[i] begins spaces[i]     */
    /*after word[i-1]*/
extern int w,   /*w=no words in line*/
            ll; /*ll is line length */

void error(char *msg);
void justify(int nch, int odd);
void printline(void);
int token(char *s);
```

The formatter starts by processing text in the fill and justify modes. It gets tokens, the pieces into which the document to be formatted is disassembled, by calling function *token*. In the fill mode, the formatter assembles a line, storing the words in the two-dimensional array *word*. Spaces between words are noted in array *spaces*. No spaces are printed before the first word or after the last word. When no more words can be put in the current line, the line is right justified (by calling function *justify*) and then printed (by calling function *printline*).

Upon encountering a new paragraph, new page, or change to no-fill mode formatting command, the output line currently being assembled is printed without right justification.

In the (no-fill) copy mode, the formatter copies the input read by it directly to the output, obeying formatting commands until it encounters the command restoring the fill mode of operation.

We will now show you the *main* function (stored in file *fmt.c*) which is the heart of the formatter program:

```c
#include "fmt.h"

char word[LL][WL];
int spaces[LL];
int w = 0, ll = 60;

/*line length (<LL) can be specified on the*/
/*command line*/

main(int argc, char *argv[])
{
  char a[WL];
  int type, n = 0, nofill = 0, sp = 0, odd =0;
      /*n == current line length*/
      /*sp == spaces between words*/

  if (argc == 2) sscanf(argv[1], "%d", &ll);
  while ((type = token(a)) != EOF) {
    switch (type) {
      case NOFILL:
        nofill = 1; printline();
        w = n = sp = 0;
        if (token(a) != NL)
           error("newline expected");
        continue;
      case FILL:
        nofill = 0;
        if (token(a) != NL)
           error("newline expected");
        continue;
      case NEWPAGE:
      case PARA:
        printline();
        putchar(type == PARA ? '\n' : '\f');
        w = n = sp = 0;
        if (token(a) != NL)
           error("newline expected");
        continue;
      default:
        ;
    }
    if (nofill) {printf("%s", a); continue;}
nextline:
    if (n + strlen(a) <= ll) {
      if (type == NL || type == SPACE) {
        if (w != 0) {n++; sp++;}
           /*no spaces before first word*/
      }
      else {
        spaces[w] = sp; sp = 0;
        strcpy(word[w++], a); n += strlen(a);
      }
    }
```

```
      else {
        justify(n-sp, odd = !odd);
          /*n-sp == total # of characters in line*/
          /*minus trailing spaces*/
        printline(); w = n = sp = 0;
        goto nextline;
      }
    }
  }
  if (w != 0)   /*flush out the last few words*/
    printline();
}
```

Notice the use of the *goto* statement. After determining that the next token will not fit on the line currently being assembled, the line is printed, and the token is then inserted in the next line. The *goto* statement is used to jump back to the code for inserting a token into a line. There is no need to get a new token because the last token still has to be processed (we will get a new token if we just continue with the next iteration of the loop). In general, the use of *goto* statements can be detrimental to program readability and understandability. Although *goto* statements can always be avoided, sometimes as in this example, their use is convenient (and appropriate). We could have avoided the use of the *goto* by using a "flag" variable.

The absence of any statements in the *NEWPAGE* alternative effectively means that both *NEWPAGE* and *PARA* are labels for the same set of statements. Note that in the *NEWPAGE* and *PARA* alternative the *continue* statement is used instead of the *break* statement to terminate execution of the *switch* statement. The *continue* statement initiates the next iteration of the surrounding loop which ensures that control does not flow on to the next alternative (*default* alternative in this case).

Function *justify* right justifies a line by inserting blanks between the words. For odd lines it starts inserting blanks from the left side of the line and for even lines it starts from the right side. Alternating the direction from which the blanks are inserted avoids "holes" from appearing in the text. Here is the function *justify* (stored in file *fmtjst.c*):

```
#include "fmt.h"

void justify(int nch, int odd)
        /*nch:no of char in line    */
        /*odd==1: odd numbered line */
        /*odd==0: even numbered line*/
{
  int i, nblnk = 11 - nch;

  i = odd ? 1 : w-1;
  while (nblnk >0) {
    spaces[i]++; nblnk--;
    if (odd)
      i = i < w-1 ? i+1 : 1;
    else
      i = i > 1 ? i-1 : w-1;
  }
}
```

Function *printline* (stored in file *fmtprtl.h*) prints the words stored in the two-dimensional array *word*, inserting spaces between the words according to the values of the elements in array *spaces*:

```
#include "fmt.h"

void printline(void)
{
  int j, k;
  for (j=0; j<w; j++) {
    for (k=0; k < spaces[j]; k++)
        putchar(' ');
    printf("%s", word[j]);
  }
  putchar('\n');
}
```

The error printing function *error* (stored in file *fmterr.c*) is straightforward:

```
#include "fmt.h"

void error(char *msg)
{
  printf("Error: %s\n", msg);
  exit(1);
}
```

Now it is time to take a look at function *token* that disassembles the input text into tokens. This function returns the token type as the function result, and it stores the token text in the address pointed to by the function parameter *s*. Character "@" is treated specially only if it begins in column one; in this case it must begin a valid formatter command. Here is the function *token* (stored in file *fmttkn.c*):

```c
#include <ctype.h>
#include "fmt.h"

int token(char *s)
        /*s: string for holding token*/
{
  int c, i;
  static int col = 0;

  while ((c = getchar()) != EOF) {
    col++;
    if (c == ' ') {
        s[0] = c; s[1] = '\0';
        return SPACE;
    }
    else if (c == '\n') {
        s[0] = c; s[1] = '\0'; col = 0;
        return NL;
    }
    else if (c == '@' && col == 1) {
        s[0] = c; s[2] = '\0';
        switch(s[1] = getchar()) {
          case 'p':
            return PARA;
          case 'n':
          case 'f':
            s[2] = getchar(); s[3] = '\0';
            if (strcmp(s, "@nf") == 0)
                return NOFILL;
            else if (strcmp(s, "@fi") == 0)
                return FILL;
            else if (strcmp(s, "@np") == 0)
                return NEWPAGE;
          default:
            fprintf(stderr,
                "token: illegal @ cmd: %s\n",s);
            exit(1);
        }
    }
    else {
        s[0] = c; i = 1;
        while(!isspace(c=getchar())) s[i++] = c;
        s[i] = '\0';
        if (c != EOF) ungetc(c, stdin);
        return WORD;
    }
  }
  return EOF;
}
```

Variable *col* is defined with the storage class *static* so that it retains its value across multiple calls to function *token*. *col* could also have been declared as an external variable in which case it would also retain its value across function calls.

However, declaring *col* as an external variable would make it visible to other functions disregarding the fact that they may have no need to access *col*. Therefore, declaring *col* as an external variable increases the chances of some function erroneously accessing or updating it.

Note that strings are compared using the library function *strcmp*. Unlike the equality operator in FORTRAN, the C equality operator = = cannot be used to compare strings because, as mentioned before, strings are not a C built-in data type. The function call *strcmp(s, t)* returns a negative, zero or positive value, depending upon whether string *s* is lexicographically less than, identical to, or greater than string *t*. Comparing two strings using the equality operator is not flagged as an error by the C compiler because C interprets it as a comparison of the pointers that refer to the beginning of the two strings. Of course, it is possible that you may sometimes fortuitously get the right result.

4. EXERCISES

1. How can you make the bank teller's program more robust? That is, catch more errors and give better diagnostics?

2. Almost all large computer operating systems, including some PC operating systems, allow multiple users to simultaneously use the computer. Can you give scenarios illustrating problems that could occur if two bank tellers try to simultaneously open a new account or update an existing account?

3. What facilities are needed to prevent two bank tellers from simultaneously updating the same bank account or preventing one bank teller from updating the account while the other is querying it?

4. What functionality can you add to the bank teller program?

5. Modify function *justify* so that it justifies a line by always inserting blanks starting from the same direction, that is, there should be no difference in justifying odd or even numbered lines. Compare the formatted output using the modified *justify* with the formatted output produced using the original definition of *justify*.

6. The formatting program does not paginate. To be specific, it just prints its output one line after another ignoring page boundaries. Therefore, it does not leave space for the customary top and bottom margins on a page. Modify the formatting program so that it leaves a few blank lines both at the top and bottom of each page.

7. Extend the formatting program with additional formatting commands such as center the next line, change indentation, stop and resume right justification, change line length, and specify alternative page sizes.

CHAPTER 8

FORTRAN FACILITIES NOT IN C

In this chapter, I will summarize the FORTRAN facilities for which there are no counterparts in C. Where appropriate, I will make comments such as how a FORTRAN facility not in C can be implemented in C or why such a facility is not necessary in C.

Here is a list of the FORTRAN facilities not in C:

- C does not have an *IMPLICIT* statement. All variables must be explicitly declared in C as a result of which there is no need for an *IMPLICIT* statement.

- Unlike FORTRAN arrays, all C arrays have the lower bound 0.

- C does not differentiate between functions and subroutines. A C function with the result type *void* is like a FORTRAN subroutine.

- C does not have a *CALL* statement. C subroutine calls are like FORTRAN subroutine calls except that the keyword *CALL* is not used.

- C does not have the counterpart of the FORTRAN *DIMENSION* statement. There is no need for such a statement in C (or even in FORTRAN) because array bounds can be specified when defining the array. Note that in FORTRAN the *DIMENSION* statement can be used in conjunction with the *IMPLICIT* statement which is not available in C.

- C does not support Hollerith constants. Such constants are not necessary if string constants can be defined. Both FORTRAN and C support string constants.

- FORTRAN prevents users from jumping inside block structures such as *DO* loops and *IF* statements (using the *GOTO* statement). C does not make such a restriction. It is up to the programmer to avoid such use.

- C does not support the type *COMPLEX*. However, a complex type can be easily built in C using structures, and appropriate functions can be provided for manipulating complex values. Unfortunately, conforming to mathematical notation is not exact; operators such as + and * cannot be extended to operate on complex values.

- C does not support subscript checking because the C philosophy has been not to support facilities that cause a run-time overhead. Unfortunately, bugs caused by out-of-bounds subscripts can be hard to find.

- C does not have a *DATA* statement. Such a statement is not needed in C because variables can be initialized in their definitions.

- C does not have a *COMMON* statement. However, the external variables of C can be used for inter-module communication much like FORTRAN's blank common variables.

C also does not have a facility corresponding to the *BLOCK DATA* statement which is used for initializing variables allocated in named common blocks.

- C does not have an *EQUIVALENCE* statement. But *union* types in C can be used to overlay storage much like the way in which *EQUIVALENCE* statements are used.

- Unlike FORTRAN, C does not have a logical type. But this is not a problem because C treats zero as false and non-zero values as true.

- C does not have an *EXTERNAL* statement, but the C *extern* storage class corresponds to the FORTRAN *EXTERNAL* statement.

- There is no need for an *INTRINSIC* statement in C. Pre-defined functions are declared and used just like ordinary user-defined functions.

- C does not have a *SAVE* statement. But the semantics of local variables with the *static* storage class correspond to the functionality provided by the FORTRAN *SAVE* statement.

- C does not have a facility corresponding to the implied-*DO* statement of FORTRAN. Such loops must be implemented by using explicit looping.

- C does not have a statement corresponding to FORTRAN's *ASSIGN* statement. The use of the *ASSIGN* statement for storing the label of a *FORMAT* statement is not needed in C because the address of the format string can be trivially stored in a variable.

- C does not have a *FORMAT* statement. Such a statement is not needed in C. The format of the items to be printed or read is specified by a string containing the appropriate formats and is supplied as an argument to the appropriate input/output function. Note that the format string can also be specified directly within the FORTRAN *READ* and *WRITE* functions, but this was not allowed in older versions of FORTRAN.

- C does not have a special facility corresponding to FORTRAN's computed *GOTO* statement. The C *switch* statement can be trivially made to yield equivalent functionality.

- C does not have a facility corresponding to the assigned *GOTO* statement in FORTRAN. This statement is not really necessary in a structured language like C which attempts to discourage the use of *GOTO* statements.

- C does not have a statement corresponding to FORTRAN's arithmetic *IF* statement (which has been made redundant by the addition of the block *IF* statement to FORTRAN). This *IF* statement results in implicit *GOTO*s. A structured language like C avoids statements because of the *GOTO*s.

- C does not have a *PAUSE* statement; such a statement can be trivially implemented by calling functions *printf* (or *fprintf*) and then *getchar* (or *fgetc*).

- C does not have a *STOP* statement. Program execution is explicitly terminated by calling function *exit*. An appropriate stopping value can be trivially printed on the console.

- Facilities corresponding to the file manipulation statements such as *BACKSPACE* and *CLOSE* of FORTRAN are supported as standard library functions just like input/output are supported by means of library functions.

- FORTRAN's formatted input/output facilities are more elaborate than those provided by C.

- C does not have a facility that corresponds to FORTRAN's statement functions. But C functions or macros can be used, instead.

- C does not support passing arguments by reference as done by FORTRAN. Arguments are passed by value. However, argument passing by reference can be simulated by passing pointers to the arguments instead of passing the arguments themselves.

- C does not support the alternative returns from FORTRAN subroutines (specified using the *RETURN* statement). These returns are really implicit *GOTO*s. This conflicts with the structured programming language design philosophy used in C which attempts to eliminate the use of *GOTO*s.

- C does not have a facility corresponding to the FORTRAN *ENTRY* statement. An *ENTRY* statement allows a function to begin executing at an executable statement other than the first one. C does not support such a facility because it complicates the semantics of the program and is not in the spirit of structured programming.

- C does not have an *END* statement. The end of a program unit is indicated by the right curly brace (which matches the opening left curly brace).

- Corresponding to the intrinsic functions, C provides standard library functions (e.g., the math library functions whose declarations are contained in the header file *math.h*). However, unlike the intrinsic functions, they are not special in any way, e.g., they do not have any generic names.

APPENDIX

C LIBRARY FUNCTIONS

C is a small and relatively simply language. Many facilities are provided as library functions; ANSI C requires each C compiler to supply standard libraries containing these functions. Typically, C compilers also provide macro versions of some functions. As discussed in Chapter 6, macros can speed up program execution time, but the storage required for the program may increase. Functions may sometimes be preferred to macros because, unlike macros, they can be passed as arguments in function calls. Also, macros can lead to unexpected results if they are invoked with arguments that have side effects. C compilers provide header files that contain prototypes of the library functions, definitions of the macro versions of library functions, and items related to the functions. Consequently, instead of writing the function prototypes explicitly, C programmers typically include the appropriate header files by using the C preprocessor #*include* instruction.

When a C compiler also provides the macro version of a library function, the same name is used for both the macro and the function. If for some reason a function is to be used instead of the equivalent macro, then the macro definition given in the header file can be removed by the preprocessor statement

`#undef` *macro-name*

Removing the macro definition forces the use of the function version. Note that this instruction should be given after the preprocessor instruction including the header file.

When describing a C library function, we will first give its specification and then discuss its functionality. The specification of a function consists of two parts:

1. Header files that must be included for using the function. These files contain the declarations and the definitions necessary for using the function.

2. The function prototype.

We will discuss the commonly used library functions which constitute most of the library functions.

1. CHARACTER PROCESSING

Character processing functions are of two kinds: *classification* and *conversion*. The classification functions, which begin with the prefix *is*, are used for determining the type of a character, e.g., *isalpha*. The conversion functions convert a lower-case letter to upper case and vice versa.

1.1 CHARACTER CLASSIFICATION

The specification of the character classification functions is of the form

```
#include <ctype.h>
int istest(int c);
```

where *test* denotes the classification performed by the function. Function *istest* returns 1 if its character argument *c* satisfies the test; otherwise it returns 0.

The following table summarizes the character classification functions:

function	classification test
isalnum	letter or digit
isalpha	letter
iscntrl	control character
isdigit	digit
isgraph	printing character (except a space)
islower	lower-case letter
isprint	printing character (including a space)
ispunct	punctuation character
isspace	white-space character (i.e., a space, carriage-return, form-feed, new-line, horizontal, or vertical-tab character)
isupper	upper-case letter
isxdigit	hexadecimal digit

1.2 CHARACTER CONVERSION

The specification of the character conversion functions is of the form

```
#include <ctype.h>
int totype(int c);
```

where *type* denotes the category to which argument *c* is to be converted. If function *totype* can perform the conversion, it returns the converted character. Otherwise, it returns *c*.

The following table summarizes the character conversion functions:

function	conversion
tolower	lower case
toupper	upper case

2. MATH

2.1 ACOS: ARC COSINE

```
#include <math.h>
double acos(double x);
```

Returns the arc cosine (between 0 and π radians) of x which must be in the range -1 to 1.

2.2 ASIN: ARC SINE

```
#include <math.h>
double asin(double x);
```

Returns the arc sine (between $-\pi/2$ and $\pi/2$ radians) of x which must be in the range -1 to 1.

2.3 ATAN: ARC TAN

```
#include <math.h>
double atan(double x);
```

Returns the arc tangent (between $-\pi$ and π). The signs of x and y determine the quadrant of the arc tangent.

2.4 COS: COSINE

```
#include <math.h>
double cos(double x);
```

Returns the cosine of its argument x which must be in radians.

2.5 TAN: TANGENT

```
#include <math.h>
double tan(double x);
```

Returns the tangent of its argument x which must be in radians.

2.6 COSH: HYPERBOLIC COSINE

```
#include <math.h>
double cosh(double x);
```

Returns the hyperbolic cosine of its argument x.

2.7 SINH: HYPERBOLIC SINE

```
#include <math.h>
double sinh(double x);
```

Returns the hyperbolic sine of its argument x.

2.8 TANH: HYPERBOLIC TAN

```
#include <math.h>
double tanh(double x);
```

Returns the hyperbolic tangent of its argument x.

2.9 EXP: EXPONENTIATION

```
#include <math.h>
double exp(double x);
```

Returns the value e^x.

2.10 FREXP: SPLIT DOUBLE VALUE INTO FRACTION & EXPONENT

```
#include <math.h>
double frexp(double v, int *xp);
```

Returns the fractional part (mantissa) of argument v and stores the exponent of v in the integer pointed to by xp. The fractional part will be zero or greater than or equal to 0.5 but less than 1.0.

2.11 LDEXP: COMBINE FRACTION & EXPONENT TO CONSTRUCT A DOUBLE VALUE

```
#include <math.h>
double ldexp(double v, int x);
```

Function *ldexp* does the opposite of *frexp*: it combines a fractional part v and an exponent x to produce a *double* value which is the value returned by *ldexp*.

2.12 LOG: NATURAL LOGARITHM

```
#include <math.h>
double log(double x);
```

Returns the natural logarithm of x.

2.13 LOG10: BASE 10 LOGARITHM

```
#include <math.h>
double log10(double x);
```

Returns the base 10 logarithm of x.

2.14 MODF: SPLIT DOUBLE VALUE

```
#include <math.h>
double modf(double x, double *ip);
```

Splits *x* into an integer part which is stored in the object pointed to by *ip* and returns the fractional part.

2.15 POW: RAISE TO A POWER

```
#include <math.h>
double pow(double x, double y);
```

Returns x^y.

2.16 SQRT: SQUARE ROOT

```
#include <math.h>
double sqrt(double x);
```

Returns the square root of *x*.

2.17 CEIL: CEILING

```
#include <math.h>
double ceil(double x);
```

Returns the next smallest integer greater than *x*.

2.18 FLOOR: FLOOR

```
#include <math.h>
double floor(double x);
```

Returns the next largest integer smaller than *x*.

2.19 FMOD: FLOATING-POINT MODULUS

```
#include <math.h>
double fmod(double x, double y);
```

Returns the fractional part of the result of dividing *x* by *y*. Functionality is essentially similar to that of the integer operator % which is not defined for *double* values.

3. NON-LOCAL JUMPS

3.1 SETJMP: SAVE ENVIRONMENT FOR LONG JUMP

```
#include <setjmp.h>
int setjmp(jmp_buf env);
```

Macro *setjmp* saves the program environment at the point of the call in the buffer *env*. It then returns 0. *longjmp* can be used to restore this environment. *longjmp* never returns; instead, calling *longjmp* using the environment saved with *setjmp* causes *setjmp* to return with a non-zero value.

3.2 LONGJMP: RESTORE SAVED ENVIRONMENT

```
#include <setjmp.h>
void longjmp(jmp_buf env, int v);
```

longjmp restores the program environment *env* saved in a previous *setjmp* call. The program then continues as if this *setjmp* call had returned the value *v*.

4. SIGNAL HANDLING

ANSI C specifies the following standard signals:

signal	condition
SIGABRT	abnormal termination
SIGFPE	zero divide or overflow
SIGILL	illegal instruction
SIGINT	interrupt
SIGSEGV	illegal memory reference
SIGTERM	termination signal

4.1 SIGNAL: SET UP A SIGNAL HANDLER

```
#include <signal.h>
void (*signal(int sig, void (*sigfun)(int))) (int);
```

signal sets up the signal handler. When signal *sig* is raised, function *sigfun* will be called with *sig* as its argument. *signal* returns the old signal handler (*SIG_ERR* in case of an error). The special pre-defined functions *SIG_IGN* and *SIG_DFL* respectively specify that the signal is to be ignored and that default action is to be taken.

4.2 RAISE: GENERATE A SIGNAL

```
#include <signal.h>
int raise(int sig);
```

Generates the signal *sig*; it returns 0 if successful and non-zero otherwise.

5. VARIABLE ARGUMENTS

These macros are used for accessing arguments of functions that can be called with a variable number of arguments. The parameter declaration (or type) list of such functions ends with a trailing ellipsis.

5.1 VA_START: STARTUP FOR ACCESSING VARIABLE ARGUMENTS

```
#include <stdarg.h>
int va_start(va_list ap, parmN);
```

Initialize *ap* for accessing the variable arguments (corresponding to the trailing ellipsis in the function header). *parmN* is the identifier representing the last parameter before the ellipsis.

5.2 VA_ARG: GET NEXT VARIABLE ARGUMENT

```
#include <stdarg.h>
type va_arg(va_list ap, type);
```

After the variable list parameter *ap* has been initialized by calling *va_start*, *va_arg* can be called to get the variable arguments. The first invocation gets the first argument, the second gets the second argument, and so on. Parameter *type* is the type of the argument being accessed.

5.3 VA_END: ENDING ACCESS OF VARIABLE NUMBER OF ARGUMENTS

```
#include <stdarg.h>
int va_end(va_list ap);
```

Macro *va_end* is called after the variable arguments have been accessed.

6. INPUT/OUTPUT

C input/output functions frequently refer to the following pre-defined constants which are defined in the header file *stdio.h*:

stdin	Standard input stream.
stdout	Standard output stream.
stderr	Standard error stream.
EOF	End-of-file value (-1).
FILE *	Type used to declare objects that refer to files.
NULL	The null pointer.

6.1 REMOVE: DELETE A FILE

```
#include <stdio.h>
int remove(const char *name);
```

Deletes the file whose name is the string pointed to by *name*. Returns 0 if successful; otherwise, non-zero.

6.2 RENAME: CHANGE FILE NAME

```
#include <stdio.h>
int rename(const char *old, const char *new);
```

Changes the name of a file: *old* points to the old file name and *new* points to the new file name. *rename* returns 0 if it is successful and non-zero otherwise.

6.3 TMPFILE: CREATE A TEMPORARY FILE

```
#include <stdio.h>
FILE *tmpfile(void);
```

Creates a temporary file and returns a pointer to the file, which is opened as a stream. *tmpfile* returns the null pointer if it is unsuccessful.

6.4 TMPNAM: GENERATE UNIQUE FILE NAME

```
#include <stdio.h>
char *tmpnam(char *fname)
```

Generates a unique file name and returns a pointer to it. If *fname* is not null, then the pointer is stored in the array pointed to by *fname* (the size of this array must be greater than or equal to the constant *L_tmpnam* which is defined in header file *stdio.h*).

6.5 FCLOSE: CLOSE STREAM

```
#include <stdio.h>
int fclose(FILE *stream)
```

Closes the stream pointed to by *stream* after flushing it and returns 0. If unsuccessful, *fclose* returns *EOF*.

Files are automatically closed upon program termination, but it is a good idea to close the files explicitly after you have finished using them. This minimizes the chances of data being lost in case of premature program termination. Also, many operating systems have a limit on the number of files that can be open at any given time.

6.6 FFLUSH: FLUSH OUTPUT BUFFER

```
#include <stdio.h>
int fflush (FILE *stream);
```

Writes to the stream pointed to by *stream* output collected in the output buffer associated with *stream* and returns 0. If unsuccessful, *fflush* returns *EOF*.

6.7 FOPEN: OPEN A FILE

```
#include <stdio.h>
FILE *fopen(const char *fname, const char *mode);
```

fopen opens the file with the name pointed to by the character pointer *fname* as a stream and returns a pointer to the stream. In case *fopen* cannot open the file it returns the null pointer *NULL*.

Argument *mode* specifies the manner in which the file will be accessed:

mode	effect
"r"	Open an existing file for reading.
"w"	Create a new file or open an existing file for writing; in the latter case mark the file as empty.
"a"	Create a new file or open an existing file for writing; in the latter case the text will be appended to the file.
"rb"	Open a binary file for reading.
"wb"	Create a new binary file or open an existing binary file for writing; in the latter case mark the file as empty.
"ab"	Create a new binary file or open an existing binary file for writing; in the latter case new data will be appended to the file.
"r+"	Open an existing file for update (reading and writing) starting from the beginning of the file.
"w+"	Create a new file or open an existing file for updating (reading and writing); in the latter case mark the file as empty.
"a+"	Create a new file or open an existing file for updating (reading and writing); in the latter case the text will be appended to the file.
"r+b"	Open an existing binary file for update (reading and writing) starting from the beginning of the file.
"w+b"	Create a new binary file or open an existing binary file for updating (reading and writing); in the latter case mark the file as empty.
"a+b"	Create a new binary file or open an existing binary file for updating (reading and writing); in the latter case data will be appended to the file.

Read and write operations for files opened for update (indicated by the character "+") must be separated by calls to *rewind* or *fseek* operations.

6.8 FREOPEN: REOPEN A FILE

```
#include <stdio.h>
FILE *freopen(const char *fname, const char *mode,
                                    FILE *stream);
```

Closes the file whose name is pointed to by *fname*, then opens the file as a stream with the access type *mode*, and associates it with the stream pointed to by *stream*. If *freopen* is successful then it returns *stream*; otherwise it returns *NULL*.

6.9 SETBUF: SET BUFFERING

```
#include <stdio.h>
void setbuf(FILE *stream, char *buf);
```

Calling *setbuf* is equivalent to the call

```
    (void) setvbuf(stream, buf, _IOFBF, BUFSIZE);
```

If *buf* is the null pointer, then calling *setbuf* is equivalent to the call

```
    (void) setvbuf(stream, NULL, _IONBF, 0);
```

6.10 SETVBUF: SET BUFFERING

```
#include <stdio.h>
int setvbuf(FILE *stream, char *buf, int mode, size_t size);
```

Sets the buffering for the stream pointed to by *stream*. If *setvbuf* is to be used to explicitly specify buffering, then it must be called after *stream* is associated with a file but before input/output is performed on the stream. If *mode* is equal to

- _IOFBF then input/output will be fully buffered;
- _IOLBF then input/output will be line buffered;
- _IONBF then input/output will not be buffered.

If *buf* is not a null pointer, then the array pointed to by *buf* (whose size is specified by the parameter *size*) is used for buffering instead of an internal buffer allocated by *setvbuf*.

6.11 FPRINTF: WRITE FORMATTED OUTPUT TO A FILE (also see PRINTF, SPRINTF, VFPRINTF, VPRINTF & VSPRINTF)

```
#include <stdio.h>
int fprintf(FILE *stream, const char *fmt, ...);
```

Function *fprintf* is similar to function *printf* with one exception: *fprintf* can be used to write to any stream (specified by the parameter *stream*) while *printf* writes just to standard output. For more details, see the description of *printf*.

6.12 FSCANF: READ FORMATTED INPUT FROM A FILE (also see SCANF & SSCANF)

```
#include <stdio.h>
int fscanf(FILE *stream, const char *fmt, ...);
```

fscanf is similar to function *scanf* with one exception: *fscanf* can be used to read from any stream (specified by the parameter *stream*) while *scanf* reads just from standard input. For more details, see the description of *scanf*.

6.13 PRINTF: WRITE FORMATTED OUTPUT TO STDOUT (also see FPRINTF, SPRINTF, VFPRINTF, VPRINTF & VSPRINTF)

```
#include <stdio.h>
int printf(const char *fmt, ...);
```

printf is used for writing formatted text to standard output. The output is written according to the format specified by the string *fmt* which contains the text to be printed and format items (also called conversion specifications). The format items specify the print formats and act as place holders for the variable number of arguments (represented by the ellipsis) which are to be printed. There must be one format in the string pointed to by item *fmt* for each one of the arguments to be printed and vice versa.

Each format item begins with the percent character and is of the form

%FlagsWidthPrecisionType

Items *Flags*, *Width*, and *Precision* are optional and may be omitted. Because of the special role of the percent character, two percent characters must be given to print a single percent character.

The optional *Flags* is a sequence of characters that modify the format specified by the other components. Zero or more flag characters can be given:

flag	effect
–	Left justify the item.
+	Print a leading sign (normally only a minus is printed).
space	Like plus, but a space is printed instead of a leading plus.
#	Prefix numbers printed with octal and hexadecimal format with a 0, 0x, or 0X. For floating-point formats, a decimal point is always printed.
0	Use leading zeros, instead of blanks, for padding.

The optional *Width* is a non-negative integer that specifies the minimum field width for the item to be printed.

The optional *Precision* is a decimal point followed by an optional integer (assumed to be zero if omitted) whose meaning depends upon the value of *Type* in the item format:

1. For integer formats (*d*, *o*, *u*, *x*, and *X*), *Precision* specifies the minimum number of digits to be printed.

2. For the floating-point format (*f*) and for the scientific formats (*e* and *E*), *Precision* specifies the number of fractional digits.

3. For the floating/scientific format (*g*), *Precision* specifies the maximum number of significant digits.

4. For the string format (*s*), *Precision* specifies the maximum number of characters to be printed.

The *Type* component specifies the actual conversion necessary to print the corresponding argument. The conversion is specified by one of the characters listed below. Note that to print *long* (*short*) arguments, the conversion character for printing integers should be preceded by the letter *l* (*h*); for *long double* arguments, the conversion character for printing *double* values should be preceded by the letter *L*:

conversion	effect
c	Print a character.
d	Print a decimal integer.
e	Print a double precision value (in scientific notation); note that *float* values are automatically converted to *double* before printing.
f	Print a double precision value; note that *float* values are automatically converted to *double* before printing.
E	Same as the conversion character *e* except that the exponent is preceded by an *E* instead of an *e*.
g	Print value in either *e* or *f* format as appropriate; the *e* format is used for very large or very small values.
o	Print an octal number.
s	Print a string.
u	Print an unsigned integer.
x	Print a hexadecimal integer.

Function *printf* returns the number of characters that are printed. If unsuccessful, it returns a negative value.

6.14 SCANF: READ FORMATTED INPUT FROM STDIN (also see FSCANF & SSCANF)

```
#include <stdio.h>
int scanf(const char *fmt, ...);
```

scanf reads data from the standard input as specified by the format string *fmt*; it stores this data in the variables whose addresses are given as arguments (represented by the ellipsis) following the format string. The format string contains four classes of items:

1. White space characters which cause input to be read up to the first non-white space character in the input.

2. Format items (also called conversion specifications), which begin with the percent character %, specifying the data format and act as place holders for the pointer arguments which specify where data is to be stored.

3. Any other character which is not part of a format item must be matched by an identical character in the input.

4. Pairs of percent characters to match a single percent character in the input.

There must be one format item in the format string for each argument following the format string. Each format item is of the form

%*Width Type

The optional asterisk specifies a suppressed conversion. That is, the item is to be read as specified by the rest of the format item, but it is not to be stored in memory. No argument is given for such an item.

Format item component *Width*, which is a non-zero unsigned decimal integer, specifies the maximum field width for the data item.

The *Type* component specifies the actual conversion necessary to read the corresponding argument. The conversion is specified by one of the characters listed below. Note that to read *long* (short) arguments the conversion character for reading integers should be preceded by the letter *l* (*h*): to read *long double* arguments, the conversion character for reading floating-point values should be preceded by the letter *L*:

conversion	effect
c	Read a character.
d	Read a decimal integer.
f	Read a double precision value (using *e*, *E*, or *g* is identical to using *f*).
o	Read an octal number.
s	Read a string; a white space terminates the string.
u	Read an unsigned integer.
x	Read a hexadecimal integer.

Function *scanf* returns the number of items read and stored in the addresses specified by the arguments given after the format string. If unsuccessful, *scanf* returns a negative value.

6.15 SPRINTF: WRITE FORMATTED OUTPUT TO A STRING (also see PRINTF, FPRINTF, VFPRINTF, VPRINTF & VSPRINTF)

```
#include <stdio.h>
int sprintf(char *s, const char * fmt, ...);
```

Function *sprintf* is similar to *printf* with one exception: *sprintf* writes to a string (specified by the parameter *s*) while *printf* writes to the standard output. A terminating null character is added at the end of string *s*. For more details, see the description of *printf*.

Note that functions *sprintf* and *sscanf* can be used to perform arbitrary type conversions. First, function *sprintf* is used to store values as text in a string; then this text is "read" as appropriate by using function *sscanf*.

6.16 SSCANF: READ FORMATTED INPUT FROM A STRING (also see SCANF & FSCANF)

```
#include <stdio.h>
int sscanf(const char *s, const char *fmt, ...);
```

Function *sscanf* is similar to function *scanf* with one exception: *sscanf* reads data from a string (specified by the parameter *s*) while *scanf* reads data from the standard input. For more details, see the description of *scanf*. As explained in the description of *sprintf*, functions *sprintf* and *sscanf* can be used to perform arbitrary type conversions.

6.17 VFPRINTF: WRITE FORMATTED OUTPUT TO A FILE (also see FPRINTF, PRINTF, SPRINTF, VPRINTF & VSPRINTF)

```
#include <stdio.h>
int vfprintf(FILE *stream, const char *fmt, va_list arg);
```

Function *vfprintf* is similar to function *fprintf* with one exception: the variable argument list denoted by the ellipsis is replaced by argument *arg* properly initialized by the *va_start* macro. *arg* contains appropriate information about the variable arguments. Function *vfprintf* allows functions called with a variable number of arguments to print these arguments by passing a *va_list* variable that has been initialized by calling *va_start*. For more details, see the description of *printf*.

6.18 VPRINTF: WRITE FORMATTED OUTPUT TO A FILE (also see FPRINTF, PRINTF, SPRINTF, VFPRINTF & VSPRINTF)

```
#include <stdio.h>
int vprintf(const char *fmt, va_list arg);
```

Function *vprintf* is similar to function *vfprintf* except that it writes to standard output. For more details, see the descriptions of *vprintf* and *printf*.

6.19 VSPRINTF: WRITE FORMATTED OUTPUT TO A FILE (also see FPRINTF, PRINTF, SPRINTF, VFPRINTF & VPRINTF)

```
#include <stdio.h>
int vsprintf(char *s, const char *fmt, va_list arg);
```

Function *vsprintf* is similar to function *vfprintf* except that it writes to a string *s*. For more details, see the descriptions of *vprintf*, *vsprintf*, and *printf*.

6.20 FGETC: GET A CHARACTER FROM A FILE (also see GETC)

fgetc is the function version of macro *getc*:

```
#include <stdio.h>
int fgetc(FILE *stream);
```

Function *fgetc* returns the next character from the stream pointed to by *stream*, unless an end-of-file is encountered in which case it returns *EOF*.

6.21 FGETS: GET A STRING FROM A FILE (also see GETS)

```
#include <stdio.h>
char *fgets(char *s, int n, FILE *stream);
```

Function *fgets* reads characters from the stream pointed to by *stream* and stores them in the memory region pointed to by *s*. Characters are read until an end-of-file or a new-line character is encountered, or *n* characters have been read. A terminating null character is then added at the end. Note that the new-line character is stored in the string.

fgets also returns *s* as its result unless an immediate end-of-file is encountered or an error occurs in which case it returns the null pointer *NULL*.

6.22 FPUTC: WRITE A CHARACTER TO A FILE (also see PUTC & PUTCHAR)

fputc is the function version of macro *putc*:

```
#include <stdio.h>
int fputc(int c, FILE *stream);
```

Writes character *c* to the stream pointed to by *stream*. If successful *fputc* returns *c*; otherwise, it returns *EOF*.

6.23 FPUTS: WRITE A STRING TO A FILE (also see PUTS)

```
#include <stdio.h>
int fputs(const char *s, FILE *stream);
```

Writes string *s* (must be terminated by a null character) to the stream pointed to by *stream*. The null character is not written. If an error occurs, function *fputs* returns *EOF*; otherwise, a non-negative value.

6.24 GETC: GET A CHARACTER FROM A FILE (also see FGETC)

getc is the macro version of function *fgetc*:

```
#include <stdio.h>
int getc(FILE *stream);
```

Macro *getc* returns the next character from the stream pointed to by *stream* unless an end-of-file is encountered in which case it returns *EOF*.

6.25 GETCHAR: GET A CHARACTER FROM STDIN

getchar is the macro version of function *fgetchar*:

```
#include <stdio.h>
int getchar(void);
```

getchar returns the next character from the standard input unless an end-of-file is encountered in which case it returns *EOF*.

6.26 GETS: GET A STRING FROM STDIN (also see FGETS)

```
#include <stdio.h>
char *gets(char *s);
```

gets reads characters from standard input and stores them in the array pointed to by *s*. Characters are read until an end-of-file or a new-line character is encountered; the new-line character is replaced by a terminating null character.

gets returns *s* as its result unless an immediate end-of-file is encountered or an error occurs, in which case it returns the null pointer *NULL*.

6.27 PUTC: WRITE A CHARACTER TO A FILE (also see FPUTC & PUTCHAR)

putc is the macro version of function *fputc*:

```
#include <stdio.h>
int putc(char c, FILE *stream);
```

Writes character *c* to stream pointed to by *stream*.

6.28 PUTCHAR: WRITE A CHARACTER TO STDOUT (also see FPUTC & PUTC)

```
#include <stdio.h>
int putchar(char c);
```

Writes character *c* to file *stdout*.

6.29 PUTS: WRITE STRING TO STDOUT (also see FPUTS)

```
#include <stdio.h>
int fputs(char *s);
```

Writes string *s* on standard output and then prints the new-line character. If an error occurs, function *fputs* returns *EOF* otherwise, 0.

6.30 UNGETC: PUSH A CHARACTER BACK INTO THE INPUT FILE

```
#include <stdio.h>
int ungetc(char c, FILE *stream);
```

ungetc "ungets", that is, pushes character *c* to the stream pointed to by *stream*. Character *c* will be the character first read by the next input operation. If successful, function *ungetc* returns the character pushed back; otherwise, it returns *EOF*. Note that successive calls to *getc* must be separated by at least one call to an input function, that is, there can be only one "pushed back" character at any given time.

6.31 FREAD: READ BLOCKS FROM A FILE

```
#include <stdio.h>
int fread(void *p, size_t size, size_t n, FILE *stream);
```

fread reads up to *n* elements, each *size_t* bytes long, from the stream pointed to by *stream* and stores them in the array pointed to by *p*. *fread* returns the number of elements read successfully.

6.32 FWRITE: WRITE BLOCKS TO A FILE

```
#include <stdio.h>
int fwrite(char *p, size_t size, size_t n, FILE *stream);
```

fwrite writes *n* elements, each *size_t* bytes long, starting at the array pointed to by *p* to the stream pointed to by *stream*. *fwrite* returns the number of elements written successfully.

6.33 FGETPOS: GET FILE POSITION

```
#include <stdio.h>
int fgetpos(FILE *stream, fpos_t *pos);
```

Stores the current file position of stream pointed to by *stream* in the object pointed to by *pos* and returns 0. If it is unsuccessful, *fgetpos* returns a non-zero value.

6.34 FSEEK: MOVE TO SPECIFIED FILE POSITION

```
#include <stdio.h>
int fseek(FILE *stream, long int offset, int whence);
```

Moves the file position indicator associated with the stream pointed to by *stream*. If *whence* is equal to *SEEK_SET* then the file position indicator is moved by *offset* characters relative to the beginning of the file. If *whence* is equal to *SEEK_CUR* then the file position indicator is moved by *offset* characters relative to its current position. If *whence* is equal to *SEEK_END* then the file position indicator is moved by *offset* characters relative to the end-of-file. *fseek* returns non-zero if it is not successful.

6.35 FSETPOS: SET FILE POSITION

```
#include <stdio.h>
int fsetpos(FILE *stream, const fpos_t *pos);
```

Sets the file position indicator associated with the stream pointed to by *stream* to the value pointed to by *pos*; this value must have been obtained by calling *getpos* on *stream*. *fsetpos* returns non-zero if unsuccessful.

6.36 FTELL: GET CURRENT FILE POSITION

```
#include <stdio.h>
long int ftell(FILE *stream);
```

Returns the position of the file position indicator associated with stream pointed to by *stream*; returns -1 if unsuccessful.

6.37 REWIND: RESET A FILE

```
#include <stdio.h>
void rewind(FILE *stream);
```

Resets the stream pointed to by *stream* to its beginning.

6.38 CLEARERR: CLEAR ERROR AND EOF INDICATION

```
#include <stdio.h>
int clearerr(FILE *stream);
```

Clears the error and end-of-file conditions associated with *stream*. See [ANSI88] for details about the setting of error and end-of-file conditions.

6.39 FEOF: END-OF-FILE CHECK

```
#include <stdio.h>
int feof(FILE *stream);
```

Returns a non-zero value if an end-of-file is encountered while reading stream pointed to by *stream*; otherwise, it returns 0.

6.40 FERROR: ERROR CHECK

```
#include <stdio.h>
int ferror(FILE *stream);
```

Returns a non-zero value if an error is encountered while reading from or writing to the stream pointed to by *stream*; otherwise, it returns 0.

6.41 PERROR: PRINT ERROR MESSAGE

```
#include <stdio.h>
void perror(int errno);
```

Prints an error message corresponding to the error number *errno*. See [ANSI88] for details about how *errno* is set.

7. GENERAL UTILITY

This library contains many functions for general use. Only the functions commonly used will be described. Please see [ANSI88] for complete details.

7.1 RAND: RANDOM NUMBER

```
#include <stdlib.h>
int rand(void);
```

Returns a random number between 0 and *RAND_MAX*.

7.2 SRAND: SET SEED FOR RANDOM NUMBER GENERATOR RAND

```
#include <stdlib.h>
int srand(unsigned int seed);
```

Sets the random number generation seed value to *seed* for the random numbers generated by *rand*. The default seed value used by *rand* is 0.

7.3 CALLOC: ALLOCATE & CLEAR MEMORY (also see MALLOC)

```
#include <stdlib.h>
void *calloc(size_t n, size_t size);
```

Allocates storage for an array of *n* elements of size *size*; all the bits of the allocated storage are set to zero. If storage can be allocated, *calloc* returns a pointer to the beginning of the allocated block of storage; otherwise, it returns the null pointer *NULL*. Typically, *size* is specified by using the *sizeof* operator.

7.4 MALLOC: ALLOCATE MEMORY (also see CALLOC)

```
#include <stdlib.h>
void *malloc(size_t size);
```

Allocates a block of memory of size *size* bytes. If successful, *malloc* returns a pointer to the beginning of this block; otherwise, it returns the null pointer *NULL*.

7.5 REALLOC: REALLOCATE MEMORY

```
#include <stdlib.h>
void *realloc(void *ptr, size_t size);
```

Takes a pointer *ptr* to a previously allocated memory block and changes the size of the memory block to *size* while preserving its contents. If necessary, the contents of the current block are copied to a new memory block of the requested size. If *size* is less than the current block size, then only the contents of first *size* bytes of this block are preserved. The pointer returned by *realloc* can be

1. equal to *ptr* indicating that the current block size was simply changed,

2. different from *ptr* indicating that a new memory block was allocated, the contents of the old block copied to the new block, and the block pointed to by the original value of *ptr* deallocated, or

3. the null pointer indicating that it was not possible to do the requested reallocation.

7.6 FREE: FREE MEMORY

```
#include <stdlib.h>
void free(void *ptr);
```

Frees (deallocates) a previously allocated memory block pointed to by *ptr*. This memory block should not have been previously deallocated and the value of *ptr* must be one that was previously returned by one of the memory allocation functions.

7.7 ABORT: RAISE ABORT SIGNAL

```
#include <stdlib.h>
void abort(void);
```

Raises the abort signal *SIGABRT*. Raising *SIGABRT* will terminate the program unless a handler has been given for it.

7.8 EXIT: TERMINATE PROGRAM

```
#include <stdlib.h>
void exit(int status);
```

Terminates the program; the value *status* is returned to the environment. Successful program execution is indicated by calling *exit* with a zero or with *EXIT_SUCCESS*; failure is indicated by calling *exit* with *EXIT_FAILURE* (typically, the value 1 is used).

7.9 GETENV: GET AN ENVIRONMENT VARIABLE

```
#include <stdlib.h>
char *getenv(const char *s);
```

Searches the environment for a string (such as an environment variable) that matches the string pointed to by s. If successful, it returns the string associated with the matched string; otherwise, it returns a null pointer.

7.10 SYSTEM: EXECUTE OPERATING SYSTEM COMMAND

```
#include <stdlib.h>
int system(char *cmd);
```

Executes the operating system command specified by the string *cmd*. The value returned is implementation dependent.

7.11 BSEARCH: BINARY SEARCH

```
#include <stdlib.h>
int *bsearch(const void *key, const void *base,
             size_t n, size_t size,
             int (*cmp)(const void *, const void *));
```

Searches an array of n elements, each of size *size*, for the object pointed to by *key*. *base* points to the address of the first element of this array which must be sorted in increasing order according to the comparison function *cmp*. Function *cmp* returns an integer greater than zero, equal to zero, or less than zero, depending upon whether *key* is less than, equal to, or greater than an array element. If *bsearch* finds a match, then it returns a pointer to the array element matched; otherwise, it returns the null pointer.

7.12 QSORT: QUICKSORT AN ARRAY

```
#include <stdlib.h>
int qsort(void *base, size_t n, size_t size
          int (*cmp)(const void *, const void *));
```

Sorts an array of n elements each of size *size*; *base* points to the address of the first element of this array. The array is sorted in increasing order according to the comparison function *cmp*. Function *cmp* returns an integer greater than zero, equal to zero or less than zero depending upon whether its first argument is less than, equal to or greater than its second argument.

7.13 ABS: ABSOLUTE VALUE

```
#include <stdlib.h>
int abs(int x);
```

Returns the absolute value of x.

7.14 DIV: INTEGER DIVIDE

```
#include <stdlib.h>
div_t div(int num, int denom);
```

Returns a structure of type *div_t* that contains the quotient and remainder of dividing *num* by *denom*. Structure *div_t* is defined as

```
typedef struct div_t {
    int quot;
    int rem;
} div_t;
```

7.15 LABS: LONG INTEGER ABSOLUTE VALUE

```
#include <stdlib.h>
long int labs(long int x);
```

Returns the absolute value of *x* (similar to *abs* except that it is used for *long int* values).

7.16 LDIV: LONG INTEGER DIVIDE

```
#include <stdlib.h>
ldiv_t ldiv(long int num, long int denom);
```

Returns a structure of type *ldiv_t* that contains the quotient and remainder of dividing *num* by *denom* (similar to *div* except that it is used for *long int* values). Structure *ldiv_t* is defined as

```
typedef struct ldiv_t {
    int quot;
    int rem;
} ldiv_t;
```

8. STRING PROCESSING

This library contains the string manipulation functions and some memory copy and compare functions. Only the commonly used string manipulation function are described here. Please see [ANSI88] for complete details.

All the string processing routines assume that strings are terminated by the null character.

8.1 STRCPY: COPY STRING

```
#include <string.h>
char *strcpy(char *d, const char *s);
```

Copies the source string (including the terminating null character) pointed to by *s* to the array pointed to by the destination pointer *d*; *strcpy* returns *d*.

Note that for the proper operation of *strcpy*, the length of the string pointed to by *d* should be greater than or equal to that of the string pointed to by *s*, and that the strings *d* and *s* should not overlap.

8.2 STRNCPY: COPY *n* CHARACTERS OF STRING

```
#include <string.h>
char *strncpy(char *d, const char *s, size_t n):
```

Copies *n* characters of the source string pointed to by *s* to the destination string pointed to by *d* and returns *d*. A terminating null character is added at the end of *d*. If *n* is greater than the length of the string pointed to by *s*, then null characters will be appended to *d* until a total of *n* characters are copied. If *n* is zero or negative, then no copy is performed.

Note that for the proper operation of *strncpy*, the length of the string pointed to by *d* should be greater than or equal to *n*, and the strings pointed to by *d* and *s* should not overlap.

8.3 STRCAT: CONCATENATE STRINGS

```
#include <string.h>
char *strcat(char *d, const char *s);
```

Concatenate (append) a copy of the source string pointed to by *s* to the end of the destination string pointed to by *d*. The terminating null character in the string pointed to by *d* is overwritten with characters from the string pointed to by *s* and a new terminating null character is added after the appended characters.

Note that for the proper operation of *strcat*, the storage allocated for the string *d* should be large enough to accommodate the additional characters being copied from the string pointed to by *s*, and that the strings pointed to by *d* and *s* should not overlap.

8.4 STRNCAT: CONCATENATE *n* CHARACTERS

```
#include <string.h>
char *strncat(char *d, char *const s, size_t n);
```

Concatenate (append) the first *n* characters of the source string pointed to by *s* to the end of destination string pointed to by *d*. The terminating null character in the string pointed to by *d* is overwritten with characters from the string pointed to by *s* and a new terminating null character added after the end of the appended characters. If *n* is greater than the length of the string pointed to by *s*, then *strncat(d, s, n)* is equivalent to *strcat(d, s)*.

Note that for the proper operation of *strncat*, the storage allocated for the string *d* should be large enough to accommodate the additional characters being copied from the string pointed to by *s*, and that the strings pointed to by *d* and *s* should not overlap.

8.5 STRCMP: COMPARE TWO STRINGS

```
#include <string.h>
int strcmp(const char *a, const char *b);
```

Returns a negative, a zero, or a positive integer value depending upon whether the string pointed to by *a* is lexicographically less than, equal to, or greater than the string pointed to by *b*.

8.6 STRNCMP: COMPARE UP TO *n* CHARACTERS OF TWO STRINGS

```
#include <string.h>
int strncmp(const char *a, const char *b, size_t n);
```

Same as *strcmp* except that at most the first *n* characters of the two strings are compared.

8.7 STRCHR: SEARCH FOR THE FIRST OCCURRENCE OF A CHARACTER

```
#include <string.h>
char *strchr(const char *s, int c);
```

If character *c* is in the string pointed to by *s*, then *strchr* returns a pointer to the first occurrence of *c*; otherwise, it returns the null pointer *NULL*. The null character terminating pointed to by *s* is also considered to be in this string.

8.8 STRCSPN: MEASURE SPAN (COUNT NUMBER) OF CHARACTERS NOT IN SET

```
#include <string.h>
size_t strcspn(const char *a, const char *b);
```

Returns the number of leading characters of the string pointed to by *a* that are not in the character set specified by the string pointed to by *b*.

8.9 STRPBRK: FIND BREAK (DELIMITING) CHARACTER IN STRING

```
#include <string.h>
char *strpbrk(const char *a, const char *b);
```

If a character from the break string pointed to by *b* occurs in the string pointed to by *a*, then a pointer to the first occurrence of this character is returned; otherwise, the null pointer *NULL* is returned.

8.10 STRRCHR: SEARCH FOR THE LAST OCCURRENCE OF A CHARACTER

```
#include <string.h>
char *strrchr(const char *s, int c);
```

Same as *strchr* except that a pointer to the last occurrence of character *c* in the string pointed to by *s* is returned.

8.11 STRSPN: MEASURE SPAN (COUNT NUMBER) OF CHARACTERS IN SET

```
#include <string.h>
int strspn(const char *a, const char *b);
```

Returns the count of the number of leading characters of the string pointed to by *a* that are in the character set specified by the string pointed to by *b*.

8.12 STRSTR: FIND SUBSTRING

```
#include <string.h>
int strstr(const char *a, const char *b);
```

Returns a pointer to the first substring in the string pointed to by *a* that matches the string *b*. If there is no such string, then *strstr* returns the null pointer *NULL*.

8.13 STRTOK: GET A TOKEN

```
#include <string.h>
char *strtok(char *a, const char *b);
```

The string pointed to by *a* is treated as a list of tokens separated by one or more of the characters in the string pointed to by *b*; these characters are called the "break" or the "delimiting" characters. To get tokens from a string pointed to by *x* with the delimiters specified in the string pointed to by *y*, first call *strtok* with arguments *x* and *y*, and then call it repeatedly with the null pointer *NULL* as the first argument and *y* still as its second argument. Each time *strtok* will return a pointer to the next token from the string pointed to by *x*. Stop calling *strtok* after it returns the null pointer which indicates that it has reached the end of the string pointed to by *x*.

8.14 STRLEN: STRING LENGTH

```
#include <string.h>
int strlen(const char *s);
```

Returns the length of the string pointed to by *s* (the terminating null character is not counted in the string length).

BIBLIOGRAPHY

[ANSI78]   American National Standard Programming Language FORTRAN (ANSI X3.9 – 1978 FORTRAN 77). American National Standards Institute, New York.

[ANSI88]   Draft Proposed American National Standard for Information Systems – Programming Language C (May 1988).

[Geha88]   Gehani, N. *C: An Advanced Introduction (ANSI C Edition)*. Computer Science Press, 1988.

[Harb84]   Harbison, S. P. and G. L. Steele, Jr. *A C Reference Manual*. Prentice-Hall, 1984.

[IBM83a]   *IBM DOS* (by Microsoft). IBM Personal Computer Language Series. Item no. 1502343.

[IBM83b]   *IBM DOS Technical Reference Manual* (by Microsoft). IBM Personal Computer Language Series. Item no. 6024125.

[Kern78]   Kernighan, B. W. and D. M. Ritchie. *The C Programming Language*. Prentice-Hall, 1978.

[Kern88]   Kernighan, B. W. and D. M. Ritchie. *The C Programming Language* (2nd Edition). Prentice-Hall, 1988.

[Knut69]   Knuth, D. E. *The Art of Computer Programming (Volume 2)*. Addison-Wesley, 1969.

[Phra83]   Phraner, R. A. Nine C compilers for the IBM PC. *Byte*, Volume 8, Number 8, August 1983.

[Plum83]   Plum, T. *Learning to Program in C*. Plum Hall, 1983.

[PCM88]   Compiling the Facts on C. *PC Magazine*, v7, no. 15, September 13, 1988.

[TurboC]   *Turbo C Reference Guide*. Borland International.

INDEX

#

#define instruction 31
#if instruction 143
#ifdef instruction 143
#include instruction 142

A

abort, function 193
abs, function 194
acos, function 175
actual arguments 6, 20
addition operator 49
ANSI C x
argument passing by reference 171
arguments 6, 20
arguments, actual 6
    command-line 4
    dummy 6
    functions accepting variable 91
    passing 6
arithmetic *IF* statement 171
array bounds 169
array elements, printing 149
array name as a pointer 119
array names 39
array parameters 37
array, 2-dimensional 147
arrays 35
arrays & pointers 117, 148
arrays, deallocating (erasing) 121
    dynamic 36, 120
asin, function 175
ASSIGN statement 170
assigned *GOTO* statement 171
assignment 7
assignment as an operator 43
assignment statement 57
assignment, simple & compound 51
associativity, operator 53
atan, function 175
automatic storage class 86

B

BACKSPACE statement 171
bank teller program example 150
binary search example 37
bit operators 50
bits, shifting 49
BLOCK DATA statement 170
break statement 80
bsearch, function 194

C

C standard, de facto x
    ANSI x
    K&R x
C, general comments about 1, 27
calculator example, pocket 12
call stack example, printing 130
CALL statement 169
calloc, function 114, 192
case sensitive 28
cast operator 43, 47, 48
casting 35
ceil, function 177
char type 33
character set 28
character type 33
character, null 38
characters, non-printing 30
    special 30
clearerr, function 191
CLOSE statement 171
combining expressions 52
comma operator 52, 57
command-line arguments 4, 92, 110
comments 13, 28
COMMON statement 170
comparison operators 50
compilation, independent 103
compiler, using the Turbo C 8
compilers, some well known C x
compiling C programs 8

COMPLEX type 169
compound statement 79
computed *GOTO* statement 16, 170
conditional compilation 143
conditional expression operator 51
conditional operator 59
constant expressions 54
constants 29, 134
constants, string 30
            symbolic 31
continue statement 80
conversion rules, usual arithmetic 43
conversions, in core (memory) 42
cos, function 175
cosh, function 175
curly braces 14, 79

D

DATA statement 170
deallocating (erasing) arrays 121
declaration of an external variable 19
declarations & definitions 76
declarations vs. definitions 1, 5
declarations, comments on explicit 7
            function 93
            redundant 153
            variable 31
decrement 44
defined operator 143
definition of an external variable 19
definitions & declarations 76
definitions vs. declarations 1, 5
definitions, variable 31
derived types 35, 69
DIMENSION statement 169
div, function 195
division operator 48
DO loop, implied 149, 170
do-while loop 85
double quotes in strings, including 31
double type 34
double-word checker example 16
dummy arguments 6, 20
dynamic arrays 36
dynamic objects 114

E

ellipsis in function declarations & headers 92
END statement 171
ENTRY statement 171
enumeration type 68
EOF, end-of-file constant 10
EQUIVALENCE statement 170
error file *stderr*, standard 61
error output file *stderr*, redirecting 63
error trapping 65
example, bank teller program 150
            binary search 37
            computing accrued interest 3
            computing the square root 85
            double-word checker 16
            dynamic storage size 121
            file copy 9
            general purpose swap routine 107
            list 115, 121
            paginator 110
            pocket calculator 12
            printing call stack 130
            queue 109
            temperature distribution 147
            text formatter 160
            tree 127
examples, sorting 108
executing C programs 8
exit, function 15, 62, 193
exp, function 176
expression 54
expression evaluation 55
expressions & statements 56
expressions, constant 54
EXTERNAL statement 170
external storage class 86
external variables 19, 86, 100

F

fclose, function 180
feof, function 191
ferror, function 192
fflush, function 181
fgetc, function 188
fgetpos, function 190
fgets, function 188
file copy example 9
file inclusion 142
file inclusion, avoiding multiple 145
file manipulation & query functions, common 65
file static storage class 86

files 91
files, header 1, 27
source 1, 27
float type 34
floating-point model 2
floating-point types 34
floor, function 177
fmod, function 177
fopen, function 181
for loop 83
for loop versatility example 53
FORMAT statement 170
formatter example, text 160
FORTRAN facilities not in C 169
fprintf, function 62, 183
fputc, function 188
fputs, function 188
fread, function 190
free, function 114, 193
freopen, function 182
frexp, function 176
fscanf, function 183
fseek, function 191
fsetbuf, function 183
fsetpos, function 191
fsetvbuf, function 183
ftell, function 191
function call 44, 94
function completion 97
function declarations 93
function definitions 91
function names as arguments 101
function prototype 20, 93
function result 97
function static class 86
function, returning from a 97
functions 60, 86, 91
functions accepting variable arguments 91
functions, communication between 100
in-line 136
parameterless 91
fundamental types 68
fwrite, function 190

G

getc, function 189
getchar, function 189
getenv, function 194
gets, function 189
global variables 100
goto statement 58
GOTO statement, assigned 171

computed 16, 170

H

header file name convention 1, 27
header files 1, 27
heap 41

I

identifiers 29
IF statement, arithmetic 171
if statement 58
if statements, nested 15
IMPLICIT statement 169
implied *DO* loop 149, 170
increment 44
initialization, variable 55
input facilities 61
input file *stdin*, standard 61
input functions, common 64
input, character-oriented 16
standard 9
I/O facilities, using the 63
input/output 4
input/output facilities, using the 63
int type 33
integer types 33
interest example, computing accrued 3
interrupt handling 104
INTRINSIC statement 170
isalnum, function 174
isalpha, function 174
iscntrl, function 174
isdigit, function 174
isgraph, function 174
islower, function 174
isprint, function 174
ispunct, function 174
isspace, function 174
isupper, function 174
isxdigit, function 174

K

K&R C x
keywords 29

L

labels 58
labs, function 195
ldexp, function 176
ldiv, function 195
left, function 40
list example 115, 121
literals 29
log, function 176
log10, function 176
logical operators 50
logical type 170
long type 33
longjmp, function 105, 178
loop statements 83
loop with a null body 50, 57

M

macros 133, 135
macros, erasing 140
main, function 92
malloc, function 114, 192
modf, function 177
multiplication operator 48

N

notation used in this book 2
NULL, null pointer 76
null character 38
null pointer *NULL* 76
null statement 56

O

operating system facilities, accessing 106
operator precedence & associativity 53
operators 42
operators, unary 46
output facilities 61
output file *stdout*, standard 61
output functions, common 64
output, character-oriented 16
            standard 9

P

paginator example 110
palindrome, function 52
parameter passing 95
parameterless functions 91
parameters 6, 20
parameters, array 37
PAUSE statement 171
perror, function 192
pointer arithmetic 115
pointers 74, 113
pointers & arrays 117, 148
pointers, *void* 113
pow, function 177
precedence, operator 53
preprocessor, C 4, 67, 133
printf, function 6, 62, 184
program execution 9
prototype, function 20, 93
putc, function 189
putchar, function 189
puts, function 190

Q

qsort, function 194
queue example 109

R

raise, function 178
rand, function 192
realloc, function 114, 193
recursion 97
remainder operator 48
remove, function 180
rename, function 180
return statement 97
returns, alternative 171
rewind, function 191
Ritchie, Dennis 1
routines, calling other language 107
running C programs 8

S

SAVE statement 170
scanf, function 6, 185
selection, structure/union component 44
set example 140
setjmp, macro 105, 178
shifting bits 49

short type 33
SIGABRT, signal 104
SIGFPE, signal 104
SIGILL, signal 104
SIGINT, signal 104
signal, function 178
signal handler, specifying a 105
signal handling 104
signals, handling 105
      raising 105
      standard 104
SIGSEGV, signal 104
SIGTERM, signal 104
SIG_DFL, special signal handler 105
SIG_IGN, special signal handler 105
sinh, function 176
sort example, bubble 108, 109
sorting examples 108
source file name convention 1, 27
source files 1, 27
sprintf, function 42, 187
sqrt, function 177
square root example, computing the 85
srand, function 192
sscanf, function 187
standard input and output 9
statement functions 171
statement termination 28
statements 56
statements & expressions 56
statements on one line, multiple 28
statements, combining 14
      grouping many statements into one 79
      long 28
static variables 99
stderr, redirecting error output file 63
      standard error file 61
stdin, standard input file 61
stdout, standard output file 61
STOP statement 171
storage allocation & deallocation 114
storage allocators 114
storage classes 86
storage size example, dynamic 121
strcat, function 196
strchr, function 197
strcmp, function 197
strcpy, function 195
strcspn, function 197
string constants 30
strings, including double quotes in 31
strings 38, 135
strlen, function 39, 198

strncat, function 196
strncmp, function 197
strncpy, function 196
strpbrk, function 197
strrchr, function 197
strspn, function 198
strstr, function 198
strtok, function 198
structure assignment 72
structure component selection 44
structure components 71
structure tags 70
structures 70
subroutines 40, 169
subscript checking 170
subscript checking in C, no 118
subscripting, array 44
subtraction operator 49
swap routine example, general purpose 107
switch statement 15, 80
system, function 106, 194

T

tags, structure 70
tan, function 175
tanh, function 176
temperature distribution example 147
termination, program 65, 106
text formatter example 160
tmpfile, function 180
tmpnam, function 180
tolower, function 175
toupper, function 175
tree example 127
Turbo C compiler 8
type definitions 67
type, array 35
      character 33
typedef statement 67
types, conversion between fund. & pointer 34
      derived 35
      floating-point 34
      fundamental 32, 68
      integer 33

U

unary operators 46
ungetc, function 190
union component selection 44
union components 73
unions 73

unsigned type 34
usual arithmetic conversion rules 43

V

va_arg, macro 179
va_end, macro 179
va_start, macro 179
variable declarations & definitions 31
variable initialization 55
variables 29
vfprintf, function 187
void pointers 113
void type 68
vprintf, function 187
vsprintf, function 188

W

while loop 83
white space characters 28